W9-BCB-339

PR
6001
.U4
D65
1979

Auden, W. H. (Wystan
Hugh), 1907-1973.

The double man

DATE			

LITERATURE & LANGUAGE DIVISION

© THE BAKER & TAYLOR CO.

THE DOUBLE MAN

BY W. H. AUDEN

Poems
On This Island
Another Time

IN COLLABORATION
WITH CHRISTOPHER ISHERWOOD

The Dog Beneath the Skin
The Ascent of F6
Journey to a War
On the Frontier

WITH LOUIS MACNEICE

Letters from Iceland

W·H·AUDEN

The Double Man

"We are, I know not how, double in ourselves,
so that what we believe we disbelieve, and
cannot rid ourselves of what we condemn."

GREENWOOD PRESS, PUBLISHERS
WESTPORT, CONNECTICUT

Library of Congress Cataloging in Publication Data

Auden, Wystan Hugh, 1907-1973.
  The double man.

    Reprint of the ed. published by Random House,
New York.
    I. Title.
PS3501.U55D6 1979   821'.9'12   79-4323
ISBN 0-313-21073-X

PR
6001
.U4
D65
1979
cp. 2

Copyright, 1941, by W. H. Auden
Copyright renewed, 1968.

First published by Random House, New York

Reprinted with the permission of The Estate of W. H. Auden

Reprinted in 1979 by Greenwood Press, Inc.
51 Riverside Avenue, Westport, CT 06880

Printed in the United States of America

10 9 8 7 6 5 4 3 2 1

LIT

TO
ELIZABETH MAYER

CONTENTS

PROLOGUE

O season of repetition and return,
Of light and the primitive visions of light
    Opened in little ponds, disturbing
    The blind water that conducts excitement.

How lucid the image in your shining well
Of a limpid day, how eloquent your streams
    Of lives without language, the cell ma-
    noevres and the molecular bustle.

O hour of images when we sniff the herb
Of childhood and forget who we are and dream
    Like whistling boys of the vast spaces
    Of the Inconsistent racing towards us

With all its appealing private detail. But
Our ways are revealing; crossing the legs
    Or resting the cheek in the hand, we
    Hide the mouths through which the Dis-
        regarded

Will always enter. For we know we're not boys
And never will be: part of us all hates life,
    And some are completely against it.
    Spring leads the truculent sailors into

11

The park, and the plump little girls, but none
Are determined like the tiny brains who found
    The great communities of summer:
    Only on battlefields, where the dying

With low voices and not very much to say
Repair the antique silence the insects broke
    In an architectural passion,
    Can night return to our cooling fibres.

O not even war can frighten us enough,
That last attempt to eliminate the Strange
    By uniting us all in a terror
    Of something known, even that's a failure

Which cannot stop us taking our walks alone,
Scared by the unknown unconditional dark,
    Down the avenues of our longing:
    For however they dream they are scattered,

Our bones cannot help reassembling themselves
Into the philosophic city where dwells
    The knowledge they cannot get out of;
    And neither a Spring nor a war can ever

So condition his ears as to keep the song
That is not a sorrow from the Double Man.
    O what weeps is the love that hears, an
    Accident occurring in his substance.

NEW YEAR LETTER

(January 1, 1940)

PART I

Under the familiar weight
Of winter, conscience and the State,
In loose formations of good cheer,
Love, language, loneliness and fear,
Towards the habits of next year,
Along the streets the people flow,
Singing or sighing as they go:
Exalté, piano, or in doubt,
All our reflections turn about
A common meditative norm,   10
Retrenchment, Sacrifice, Reform.

Twelve months ago in Brussels, I
Heard the same wishful-thinking sigh
As round me, trembling on their beds,
Or taut with apprehensive dreads,
The sleepless guests of Europe lay
Wishing the centuries away,
And the low mutter of their vows
Went echoing through her haunted house,
As on the verge of happening   20
There crouched the presence of The Thing.
All formulas were tried to still
The scratching on the window-sill,
All bolts of custom made secure

Against the pressure on the door,
But up the staircase of events
Carrying his special instruments,
To every bedside all the same
The dreadful figure swiftly came.

Yet Time can moderate his tone   30
When talking to a man alone,
And the same sun whose neutral eye
All florid August from the sky
Had watched the earth behave and seen
Strange traffic on her brown and green,
Obedient to some hidden force
A ship abruptly change her course,
A train make an unwonted stop,
A little crowd smash up a shop,
Suspended hatreds crystallize   40
In visible hostilities,
Vague concentrations shrink to take
The sharp crude patterns generals make,
The very morning that the war
Took action on the Polish floor,
Lit up America and on
A cottage in Long Island shone
Where Buxtehude as we played
One of his *passacaglias* made
Our minds a *civitas* of sound   50
Where nothing but assent was found,
For art had set in order sense
And feeling and intelligence,
And from its ideal order grew
Our local understanding too.

To set in order—that's the task
Both Eros and Apollo ask;
For Art and Life agree in this
That each intends a synthesis,
That order which must be the end   60
That all self-loving things intend
Who struggle for their liberty,
Who use, that is, their will to be.
Though order never can be willed
But is the state of the fulfilled,
For will but wills its opposite
And not the whole in which they fit,
The symmetry disorders reach
When both are equal each to each,
Yet in intention all are one,   70
Intending that their wills be done
Within a peace where all desires
Find each in each what each requires,
A true *Gestalt* where indiscrete
Perceptions and extensions meet.
Art in intention is nemesis
But, realized, the resemblance ceases;
Art is not life and cannot be
A midwife to society.
For art is a *fait accompli*.   80
What they should do, or how or when
Life-order comes to living men
It cannot say, for it presents
Already lived experience
Through a convention that creates
Autonomous completed states.

Though their particulars are those
That each particular artist knows,
Unique events that once took place
Within a unique time and space,   90
In the new field they occupy,
The unique serves to typify,
Becomes, though still particular,
An algebraic formula,
An abstract model of events
Derived from dead experiments,
And each life must itself decide
To what and how it be applied.

Great masters who have shown mankind
An order it has yet to find,   100
What if all pedants say of you
As personalities be true?
All the more honor to you then
If, weaker than some other men,
You had the courage that survives
Soiled, shabby, egotistic lives,
If poverty or ugliness,
Ill-health or social unsuccess
Hunted you out of life to play
At living in another way;   110
Yet the live quarry all the same
Were changed to huntsmen in the game,
And the wild furies of the past,
Tracked to their origins at last,
Trapped in a medium's artifice,
To charity, delight, increase.
Now large, magnificent, and calm,

Your changeless presences disarm
The sullen generations, still
The fright and fidget of the will,   120
And to the growing and the weak
Your final transformation speak,
Saying to dreaming 'I am deed.'
To striving 'Courage, I succeed.'
To mourning 'I remain. Forgive.'
And to becoming 'I am. Live.'

They challenge, warn and witness. Who
That ever has the rashness to
Believe that he is one of those
The greatest of vocations chose,   130
Is not perpetually afraid
That he's unworthy of his trade,
As round his tiny homestead spread
The grand constructions of the dead,
Nor conscious, as he works, of their
Complete uncompromising stare,
And the surveillance of a board
Whose warrant cannot be ignored?
O often, often must he face,
Whether the critics blame or praise,   140
Young, high-brow, popular or rich,
That summary tribunal which
In a perpetual session sits,
And answer, if he can, to its
Intense interrogation. Though
Considerate and mild and low
The voices of the questioners,
Although they delegate to us

Both prosecution and defence,
Accept our rules of evidence   150
And pass no sentence but our own,
Yet, as he faces them alone,
O who can show convincing proof
That he is worthy of their love?
Who ever rose to read aloud
Before that quiet attentive crowd
And did not falter as he read,
Stammer, sit down, and hang his head?
Each one, so liberal is the law,
May choose whom he appears before,   160
Pick any influential ghost
From those whom he admires the most.
So, when my name is called, I face,
Presiding coldly on my case,
That lean hard-bitten pioneer
Who spoiled a temporal career
And to the supernatural brought
His passion, senses, will and thought,
By Amor Rationalis led
Through the three kingdoms of the dead,   170
In concrete detail saw the whole
Environment that keeps the soul,
And grasped in its complexity
The Catholic ecology,
Described the savage fauna he
In Malebolge's fissure found,
And fringe of blessed flora round
A juster nucleus than Rome,
When love had its creative home.
Upon his right appears, as I   180

20

Reluctantly must testify
And weigh the sentence to be passed,
A choleric enthusiast,
Self-educated WILLIAM BLAKE,
Who threw his spectre in the lake,
Broke off relations in a curse
With the Newtonian Universe,
But even as a child would pet
The tigers Voltaire never met,   189
Took walks with them through Lambeth, and
Spoke to Isaiah in the Strand,
And heard inside each mortal thing
Its holy emanation sing.
While to his left upon the bench,
Muttering that terror is not French,
Frowns the young RIMBAUD guilt demands,
The adolescent with red hands,
Skillful, intolerant and quick,
Who strangled an old rhetoric.
The court is full; I catch the eyes   200
Of several I recognize,
For as I look up from the dock
Embarrassed glances interlock.
There DRYDEN sits with modest smile,
The master of the middle style,
Conscious CATULLUS who made all
His gutter-language musical,
Black TENNYSON whose talents were
For an articulate despair,
Trim, dualistic BAUDELAIRE,   210
Poet of cities, harbors, whores,
Acedia, gaslight and remorse,

21

HARDY whose Dorset gave much joy
To one unsocial English boy,
And RILKE whom *die Dinge* bless,
The Santa Claus of loneliness.
And many others, many times,
For I relapse into my crimes,
Time and again have slubbered through
With slip and slapdash what I do,   220
Adopted what I would disown,
The preacher's loose immodest tone;
Though warned by a great sonneteer
Not to sell cheap what is most dear,
Though horrible old KIPLING cried
'One instant's toil to Thee denied
Stands all eternity's offence,'
I would not give them audience.
Yet still the weak offender must
Beg still for leniency and trust   230
His power to avoid the sin
Peculiar to his discipline.

The situation of our time
Surrounds us like a baffling crime.
There lies the body half-undressed,
We all had reason to detest,
And all are suspects and involved
Until the mystery is solved
And under lock and key the cause
That makes a nonsense of our laws.   240
O Who is trying to shield Whom?
Who left a hairpin in the room?
Who was the distant figure seen

22

Behaving oddly on the green?
Why did the watchdog never bark?
Why did the footsteps leave no mark?
Where were the servants at that hour?
How did a snake get in the tower?
Delayed in the democracies   250
By departmental vanities,
The rival sergeants run about
But more to squabble than find out,
Yet where the Force has been cut down
To one inspector dressed in brown,
He makes the murderer whom he pleases
And all investigation ceases.
Yet our equipment all the time
Extends the area of the crime
Until the guilt is everywhere,
And more and more we are aware,   260
However miserable may be
Our parish of immediacy,
How small it is, how, far beyond,
Ubiquitous within the bond
Of one impoverishing sky,
Vast spiritual disorders lie.
Who, thinking of the last ten years,
Does not hear howling in his ears
The Asiatic cry of pain,
The shots of execution Spain   270
See stumbling through his outraged mind
The Abyssinian, blistered, blind,
The dazed uncomprehending stare
Of the Danubian despair,
The Jew wrecked in the German cell,

Flat Poland frozen into hell,
The silent dumps of unemployed
Whose *arête* has been destroyed,
And will not feel blind anger draw
His thoughts towards the Minotaur,   280
To take an early boat for Crete
And rolling, silly, at its feet
Add his small tidbit to the rest?
It lures us all; even the best,
Les hommes de bonne volonté, feel
Their politics perhaps unreal
And all they have believed untrue,
Are tempted to surrender to
The grand apocalyptic dream
In which the persecutors scream
As on the evil Aryan lives   290
Descends the night of the long knives;
The bleeding tyrant dragged through all
The ashes of his capitol

Though language may be useless, for
No words men write can stop the war
Or measure up to the relief
Of its immeasurable grief,
Yet truth, like love and sleep, resents
Approaches that are too intense,   300
And often when the searcher stood
Before the Oracle, it would
Ignore his grown-up earnestness
But not the child of his distress,
For through the Janus of a joke
The candid psychopompos spoke.

May such heart and intelligence
As huddle now in conference
Whenever an impasse occurs
Use the good offices of verse;   310
May an Accord be reached, and may
This *aide-mémoire* on what they say,
This private minute for a friend,
Be the dispatch that I intend;
Although addressed to a Whitehall
Be under Flying Seal to all
Who wish to read it anywhere,
And, if they open it, *En Clair*.

PART II

Tonight a scrambling decade ends,
And strangers, enemies and friends   320
Stand once more puzzled underneath
The signpost on the barren heath
Where the rough mountain track divides
To silent valleys on all sides,
Endeavoring to decipher what
Is written on it but cannot,
Nor guess in what direction lies
The overhanging precipice.
Through the pitch-darkness can be heard
Occasionally a muttered word,   330
And intense in the mountain frost
The heavy breathing of the lost;
Far down below them whence they came
Still flickers feebly a red flame,
A tiny glow in the great void
Where an existence was destroyed;
And now and then a nature turns
To look where her whole system burns
And with a last defiant groan
Shudders her future into stone.   340

How hard it is to set aside
Terror, concupiscence and pride,
Learn who and where and how we are,

The children of a modest star,
Frail, backward, clinging to the granite
Skirts of a sensible old planet,
Our placid and suburban nurse
In SITTER's swelling universe,
How hard to stretch imagination
To live according to our station.   350
For we are all insulted by
The mere suggestion that we die
Each moment and that each great I
Is but a process in a process
Within a field that never closes;
As proper people find it strange
That we are changed by what we change,
That no event can happen twice
And that no two existences
Can ever be alike; we'd rather   360
Be perfect copies of our father,
Prefer our *idées fixes* to be
True of a fixed Reality.
No wonder, then, we lose our nerve
And blubber when we should observe
The patriots of an old idea
No longer sovereign this year,
Get angry like LABELLIÈRE,
Who, finding no invectives hurled
Against a topsy-turvy world   370
Would right it, earn a quaint renown
By being buried upside-down;
Unwilling to adjust belief,
Go mad in a fantastic grief
Where no adjustment need be done,

27

Like SARAH WHITEHEAD, the Bank Nun,
For, loving a live brother, she
Wed an impossibility,
Pacing Threadneedle Street in tears,
She watched one door for twenty years   380
Expecting what she dared not doubt,
Her hanged embezzler to walk out.

But who, though, is the Prince of Lies
If not the Spirit-that-denies,
The shadow just behind the shoulder
Claiming it's wicked to grow older
Though we are lost if we turn round
Thinking salvation has been found?
Yet in his very effort to
Prevent the actions we could do,   390
He has to make the here and now
As marvelous as he knows how
And so engrossing we forget
To drop attention for regret;
Defending relaxation, he
Mush show impassioned energy,
And all through tempting us to doubt
Point us the way to find truth out.
Poor cheated MEPHISTOPHELES,
Who think you're doing as you please   400
In telling us by doing ill
To prove that we possess free will,
Yet do not will the will you do,
For the Determined uses you,
Creation's errand-boy creator,
Diabolus egredietur

Ante pedes ejus—foe,
But so much more effective, though,
Than our well-meaning stupid friends
In driving us towards good ends.   410
Lame fallen shadow, *retro me,*
Retro but do not go away:
Although, for all your fond insistence,
You have no positive existence,
Are only a recurrent state
Of fear and faithlessness and hate,
That takes on from becoming me
A legal personality,
Assuming your existence is
A rule-of-thumb hypostasis,   420
For, though no person, you can damn,
So, *credo ut intelligam.*
For how could we get on without you
Who give the *savoir-faire* to doubt you
And keep you in your proper place,
Which is, to push us into grace?

Against his paralyzing smile
And honest realistic style
Our best protection is that we
In fact live in eternity.   430
The sleepless counter of our breaths
That chronicles the births and deaths
Of pious hopes, the short careers
Of dashing promising ideas,
Each congress of the Greater Fears,
The emigration of beliefs,
The voyages of hopes and griefs,

29

Has no direct experience
Of discontinuous events,
And all our intuitions mock   440
The formal logic of the clock.
All real perception, it would seem,
Has shifting contours like a dream,
Nor have our feelings ever known
Any discretion but their own.
Suppose we love, not friends or wives,
But certain patterns in our lives,
Effects that take the cause's name,
Love cannot part them all the same;
If in this letter that I send   450
I write 'Elizabeth's my friend,'
I cannot but express my faith
That I is Not-Elizabeth.
For though the intellect in each
Can only think in terms of speech
We cannot practise what we preach.
The cogitations of DESCARTES
Are where all sound semantics start;
In Ireland the great BERKELEY rose
To add new glories to our prose,   460
But when in the pursuit of knowledge,
Risking the future of his college,
The bishop hid his anxious face,
'Twas more by grammar than by grace
His modest Church-of-England God
Sustained the fellows and the quad.

But the Accuser would not be
In his position, did not he,

Unlike the big-shots of the day,
Listen to what his victims say.
Observing every man's desire
To warm his bottom by the fire
And state his views on Education,
Art, Women, and The Situation,
Has learnt what every woman knows,
The wallflower can become the rose,
Penelope the homely seem
The Helen of Odysseus' dream
If she will look as if she were
A fascinated listener,   480
Since men will pay large sums to whores
For telling them they are not bores.
So when with overemphasis
We contradict a lie of his,
The great Denier won't deny
But purrs: 'You're cleverer than I;
Of course you're absolutely right,
I never saw it in that light.
I see it now: The intellect
That parts the Cause from the Effect   490
And thinks in terms of Space and Time
Commits a legalistic crime,
For such an unreal severance
Must falsify experience.
Could one not almost say that the
Cold serpent on the poisonous tree
Was *l'esprit de géométrie,*
That Eve and Adam till the Fall
Were totally illogical,
But as they tasted of the fruit   500

The syllogistic sin took root?
Abstracted, bitter refugees,
They fought over their premises,
Shut out from Eden by the bar
And Chinese Wall of *Barbara.*
O foolishness of man to seek
Salvation in an *ordre logique!*
O cruel intellect that chills
His natural warmth until it kills
The roots of all togetherness!   510
Love's vigor shrinks to less and less,
On sterile acres governed by
Wage's abstract prudent tie
The hard self-conscious particles
Collide, divide like numerals
In knock-down drag-out *laissez-faire,*
And build no order anywhere.
O when will men show common sense
And throw away intelligence,
That killjoy which discriminates,   520
Recover what appreciates,
The deep unsnobbish instinct which
Alone can make relation rich,
Upon the *Beischlaf* of the blood
Establish a real neighborhood
Where art and industry and *mœurs*
Are governed by an *ordre du cœur?*

The Devil, as is not surprising—
His business is self-advertising—
Is a first-rate psychologist   530
Who keeps a conscientious list,

To help him in his ticklish deals,
Of what each client thinks and feels,
His school, religion, birth and breeding,
Where he has dined and what he's reading,
By every name he makes a note
Of what quotations to misquote,
And flings at every author's head
Something a favorite author said.
'The Arts? Well, FLAUBERT didn't say 540
Of *artists: "Ils sont dans le vrai."*
Democracy? Ask BAUDELAIRE:
"Un esprit Belge," a soiled affair
Of gas and steam and table-turning.
Truth? ARISTOTLE was discerning:
"In crowds I am a friend of myth." '
Then, as I start protesting, with
The air of one who understands
He puts a RILKE in my hands.
'You know the *Elegies,* I'm sure— 550
O Seligkeit der Kreatur
Die immer bleibt in Schoosse—womb,
In English, is a rhyme to tomb.'
He moves on tiptoe round the room,
Turns on the radio to mark
Isolde's *Sehnsucht* for the dark.

But all his tactics are dictated
By problems he himself created,
For as the great schismatic who
First split creation into two 560
He did what it could never do,
Inspired it with the wish to be

33

Diversity in unity,
An action which has put him in,
Pledged as he is to Rule-by-Sin,
As ambiguous a position
As any Irish politician,
For, torn between conflicting needs,
He's doomed to fail if he succeeds,   570
And his neurotic longing mocks
Him with its self-made paradox
To be both god and dualist.
For, if dualities exist,
What happens to the god? If there
Are any cultures anywhere
With other values than his own,
How can it possibly be shown
That his are not subjective or
That all life is a state of war?
While, if the monist view be right,   580
How is it possible to fight?
If love has been annihilated
There's only hate left to be hated.
To say two different things at once,
To wage offensives on two fronts,
And yet to show complete conviction,
Requires the purpler kinds of diction,
And none appreciate as he
Polysyllabic oratory.
All vague idealistic art   590
That coddles the uneasy heart
Is up his alley, and his pigeon
The woozier species of religion,
Even a novel, play or song,

If loud, lugubrious and long;
He knows the bored will not unmask him
But that he's lost if someone ask him
To come the hell in off the links
And say exactly what he thinks.
To win support of any kind   600
He has to hold before the mind
Amorphous shadows it can hate,
Yet constantly postpone the date
Of what he's made The Grand Attraction,
Putting an end to them by action
Because he knows, were he to win,
Man could do evil but not sin.
To sin is to act consciously
Against what seems necessity,
A possibility cut out   610
In any world that excludes doubt.
So victory could do no more
Than make us what we were before,
Beasts with a Rousseauistic charm
Unconscious we were doing harm.
Politically, then, he's right
To keep us shivering all night,
Watching for dawn from Pisgah's height,
And to sound earnest as he paints
The new Geneva of the saints,   620
To strike the poses as he speaks
Of David's too too Empire Greeks,
Look forward with the cheesecake air
Of one who crossed the Delaware.
A realist, he has always said:
'It is Utopian to be dead,

35

For only on the Other Side
Are Absolutes all satisfied
Where, at the bottom of the graves,
Low Probability behaves.'   630

The False Association is
A favorite strategy of his:
Induce men to associate
Truth with a lie, then demonstrate
The lie and they will, in truth's name,
Treat babe and bath-water the same,
A trick that serves him in good stead
At all times. It was thus he led
The early Christians to believe
All Flesh unconscious on the eve   640
Of the Word's temporal interference
With the old Adam of Appearance;
That almost any moment they
Would see the trembling consuls pray,
Knowing that as their hope grew less
So would their heavenly worldliness,
Their early agapë decline
To a late lunch with Constantine.
Thus WORDSWORTH fell into temptation
In France during a long vacation,   650
Saw in the fall of the Bastille
The Parousia of liberty,
And weaving a platonic dream
Round a provisional régime
That sloganized the Rights of Man,
A liberal fellow-traveler ran
With Sans-culotte and Jacobin,

Nor guessed what circles he was in,
But ended as the Devil knew
An earnest Englishman would do,   660
Left by Napoleon in the lurch,
Supporting the Established Church,
The Congress of Vienna and
The Squire's paternalistic hand.

Like his, our lives have been coeval
With a political upheaval,
Like him, we had the luck to see
A rare discontinuity,
Old Russia suddenly mutate
Into a proletarian state,   670
The odd phenomenon, the strange
Event of qualitative change.
Some dreamed, as students always can,
It realized the potential Man,
A higher species brought to birth
Upon a sixth part of the earth,
While others settled down to read
The theory that forecast the deed
And found their humanistic view
In question from the German who,   680
Obscure in gaslit London, brought
To human consciousness a thought
It thought unthinkable, and made
Another consciousness afraid.
What if his hate distorted? Much
Was hateful that he had to touch.
What if he erred? He flashed a light
On facts where no one had been right.

The father-shadow that he hated
Weighed like an Alp; his love, frustrated,   690
Negating as it was negated,
Burst out in boils; his animus
Outlawed him from himself; but thus,
And only thus, perhaps, could he
Have come to his discovery.
Heroic charity is rare;
Without it, what except despair
Can shape the hero who will dare
The desperate catabasis
Into the snarl of the abyss   700
That always lies just underneath
Our jolly picnic on the heath
Of the agreeable, where we bask,
Agreed on what we will not ask,
Bland, sunny and adjusted by
The light of the accepted lie?
As he explored the muttering tomb
Of a museum reading room,
The Dagon of the General Will
Fell in convulsions and lay still;   710
The tempting Contract of the rich,
Revealed as an abnormal witch,
Fled with a shriek, for as he spoke
The justifying magic broke;
The garden of the Three Estates
Turned desert, and the Ivory Gates
Of Pure Idea to gates of horn
Through which the Governments are born.
But his analysis reveals

The other side to Him-who-steals   720
Is He-who-makes-what-is-of-use,
Since, to consume, man must produce;
By Man the Tough Devourer sets
The nature his despair forgets
Of Man Prolific since his birth,
A race creative on the earth,
Whose love of money only shows
That in his heart of hearts he knows
His love is not determined by
A personal or tribal tie   730
Or color, neighborhood, or creed,
But universal, mutual need;
Loosed from its shroud of temper, his
Determinism comes to this:
None shall receive unless they give;
All must coöperate to live.
Now he is one with all of those
Who brought an epoch to a close,
With him who ended as he went
Past an archbishop's monument   740
The slaveowners' mechanics, one
With the ascetic farmer's son
Who, while the Great Plague ran its course,
Drew up a Roman code of Force,
One with the naturalist, who fought
Pituitary headaches, brought
Man's pride to heel at last and showed
His kinship with the worm and toad,
And Order as one consequence
Of the unfettered play of Chance.   750

39

Great sedentary Caesars who
Have pacified some dread tabu,
Whose wits were able to withdraw
The *numen* from some local law
And with a single concept brought
Some ancient rubbish heap of thought
To rational diversity,
You are betrayed unless we see
No *codex gentium* we make   760
It is difficult for Truth to break;
The *Lex Abscondita* evades
The vigilantes in the glades;
Now here, now there, one leaps and cries
'I've got her and I claim the prize,'
But when the rest catch up, he stands
With just a torn blouse in his hands.

We hoped; we waited for the day
The State would wither clean away,
Expecting the Millennium
That theory promised us would come,   770
It didn't. Specialists must try
To detail all the reasons why;
Meanwhile at least the layman knows
That none are lost so soon as those
Who overlook their crooked nose,
That they grow small who imitate
The mannerisms of the great,
Afraid to be themselves, or ask
What acts are proper to their task,
And that a tiny trace of fear   780
Is lethal in man's atmosphere.

The rays of Logos take effect,
But not as theory would expect,
For, sterile and diseased by doubt,
The dwarf mutations are thrown out
From Eros' weaving centrosome.

O Freedom still is far from home,
For Moscow is as far as ROME
Or PARIS. Once again we wake
With swimming heads and hands that shake   790
And stomachs that keep nothing down.
Here's where the devil goes to town
Who knows that nothing suits his book
So well as the hang-over look,
That few drunks feel more awful than
The Simon-pure Utopian.
He calls at breakfast in the rôle
Of blunt but sympathetic soul:
'Well, how's our Socialist this morning?
I could say "Let this be a warning,"   800
But no, why should I? Students must
Sow their wild oats at times or bust.
Such things have happened in the lives
Of all the best Conservatives.
I'll fix you something for your liver.'
And thus he sells us down the river.
Repenting of our last infraction
We seek atonement in reaction
And cry, nostalgic like a whore,
"I was a virgin still at four."   810
Perceiving that by sailing near
The Hegelian whirlpool of Idea

41

Some foolish aliens have gone down,
Lest our democracy should drown
We'd wreck her on the solid rock
Of genteel anarchists like Locke,
Wave at the mechanized barbarian
The vorpal sword of an Agrarian.

O how the devil who controls
The moral assymetric souls   820
The either-ors, the mongrel halves
Who find truth in a mirror, laughs.
Yet time and memory are still
Limiting factors on his will;
He cannot always fool us thrice,
For he may never tell us lies,
Just half-truths we can synthesize.
So, hidden in his hocus-pocus,
There lies the gift of double focus,
That magic lamp which looks so dull
And utterly impractical   830
Yet, if Aladdin use it right,
Can be a sesame to light.

PART III

Across East River in the night
Manhattan is ablaze with light.
No shadow dares to criticize
The popular festivities,
Hard liquor causes everywhere
A general *détente,* and Care
For this state function of Good Will   840
Is diplomatically ill:
The Old Year dies a noisy death.

Warm in your house, Elizabeth,
A week ago at the same hour
I felt the unexpected power
That drove our ragged egos in
From the dead-ends of greed and sin
To sit down at the wedding feast,
Put shining garments on the least,
Arranged us so that each and all,   850
The erotic and the logical,
Each felt the *placement* to be such
That he was honored overmuch,
And SCHUBERT sang and MOZART played
And GLUCK and food and friendship made
Our privileged community
That real republic which must be

43

The State all politicians claim,
Even the worst, to be their aim.

O but it happens every day   860
To someone. Suddenly the way
Leads straight into their native lands,
The *temenos'* small wicket stands
Wide open, shining at the centre
The well of life, and they may enter.
Though compasses and stars cannot
Direct to that magnetic spot,
Nor Will nor willing-not-to-will,
For there is neither good nor ill,
But free rejoicing energy.   870
Yet anytime, how casually,
Out of his organized distress
An accidental happiness,
Catching man off his guard, will blow him
Out of his life in time to show him
The field of Being where he may,
Unconscious of Becoming, play
With the Eternal Innocence
In unimpeded utterance.
But perfect Being has ordained   880
It must be lost to be regained,
And in its orchards grow the tree
And fruit of human destiny,
And man must eat it and depart
At once with gay and grateful heart,
Obedient, reborn, re-aware;
For, if he stop an instant there,
The sky grows crimson with a curse,

The flowers change color for the worse,
He hears behind his back the wicket   890
Padlock itself, from the dark thicket
The chuckle with no healthy cause,
And, helpless, sees the crooked claws
Emerging into view and groping
For handholds on the low round coping,
As Horror clambers from the well:
For he has sprung the trap of Hell.

Hell is the being of the lie
That we become if we deny
The laws of consciousness and claim   900
Becoming and Being are the same,
Being in time, and man discrete
In will, yet free and self-complete;
Its fire the pain to which we go
If we refuse to suffer, though
The one unnecessary grief
Is the vain craving for relief,
When to the suffering we could bear
We add intolerable fear,
Absconding from remembrance, mocked   910
By our own partial senses, locked
Each in a stale uniqueness, lie
Time-conscious for eternity.

We cannot, then, will Heaven where
Is perfect freedom; our wills there
Must lose the will to operate.
But will is free not to negate
Itself in Hell; we're free to will

Ourselves up Purgatory still,
Consenting parties to our lives,   920
To love them like attractive wives
Whom we adore but do not trust,
Who cannot love without their lust,
And need their stratagems to win
Truth out of Time. In Time we sin.
But Time is sin and can forgive;
Time is the life in which we live
At least three quarters of our time,
The purgatorial hill we climb,
Where any skyline we attain   930
Reveals a higher ridge again.
Yet since, however much we grumble,
However painfully we stumble,
Such mountaineering all the same
Is, it would seem, the only game
At which we show a natural skill,
The hardest exercises still
Just those our muscles are the best
Adapted to, its grimmest test
Precisely what our fear suspected,   940
We have no cause to look dejected
When, wakened from a dream of glory,
We find ourselves in Purgatory,
Back on the same old mountain side
With only guessing for a guide.
To tell the truth, although we stifle
The feeling, are we not a trifle
Relieved to wake on its damp earth?
It's been our residence since birth,
Its inconveniences are known,   950

46

And we have made its flaws our own.
Is it not here that we belong,
Where everyone is doing wrong,
And normal our freemartin state,
Half angel and half *petite bête?*
So, perched upon the sharp arête,
When if we do not move we fall,
Yet movement is heretical,
Since over its ironic rocks
No route is truly orthodox,   960
O once again let us set out,
Our faith well balanced by our doubt,
Admitting every step we make
Will certainly be a mistake,
But still believing we can climb
A little higher every time,
And keep in order, that we may
Ascend the penitential way
That forces our wills to be free,
A reverent frivolity   970
That suffers each unpleasant test
With scientific interest,
And finds romantic, *faute de mieux,*
Its sad *nostalgie des adieux.*

Around me, pausing as I write,
A tiny object in the night,
Whichever way I look, I mark
Importunate along the dark
Horizon of immediacies
The flares of desperation rise   980
From signalers who justly plead

47

Their cause is piteous indeed:
Bewildered, how can I divine
Which is my true Socratic Sign,
Which of these calls to conscience is
For me the *casus fœderis,*
From all the tasks submitted, choose
The *athlon* I must not refuse?
A particle, I must not yield
To particles who claim the field,   990
Nor trust the demagogue who raves,
A quantum speaking for the waves,
Nor worship blindly the ornate
Grandezza of the Sovereign State.
Whatever wickedness we do
Need not be, orators, for you;
We can at least serve other ends,
Can love the *polis* of our friends
And pray that loyalty may come
To serve mankind's *imperium.*   1000

But why and where and when and how?
O none escape these questions now:
The future which confronts us has
No likeness to that age when, as
Rome's huggermugger unity
Was slowly knocked to pieces by
The uncoördinated blows
Of artless and barbaric foes,
The stressed and rhyming measures rose;
The cities we abandon fall   1010
To nothing primitive at all;
This lust in action to destroy

Is not the pure instinctive joy
Of animals, but the refined
Creation of machines and mind.
We face our self-created choice
As out of Europe comes a voice,
A theologian who denies
What more than twenty centuries
Of Europe have assumed to be   1020
The basis of civility,
Our evil *Daimon* to express
In all its ugly nakedness
What none before dared say aloud,
The metaphysics of the Crowd,
The Immanent Imperative
By which the lost and injured live
In mechanized societies
Where natural intuition dies,
The hitherto-unconscious creed   1030
Of little men who half succeed,
The international result
Of Industry's *Quicunque vult.*

Yet maps and languages and names
Have meaning and their proper claims.
There are two atlases: the one
The public space where acts are done,
In theory common to us all,
Where we are needed and feel small,
The *agora* of work and news
Where each one has the right to choose   1040
His trade, his corner and his way,
And can, again in theory, say

For whose protection he will pay,
And loyalty is help we give
The place where we prefer to live;
The other is the inner space
Of private ownership, the place
That each of us is forced to own,
Like his own life from which it's grown,   1050
The landscape of his will and need
Where he is sovereign indeed,
The state created by his acts
Where he patrols the forest tracts
Planted in childhood, farms the belt
Of doings memorized and felt,
And even if he find it hell
May neither leave it nor rebel.
Two worlds describing their rewards,
That one in tangents, this in chords;   1060
Each lives in one, all in the other,
Here all are kings, there each a brother:
In politics the Fall of Man
From natural liberty began
When, loving power or sloth, he came
Like BURKE to think them both the same.

England to me is my own tongue,
And what I did when I was young.
If now, two aliens in New York,
We meet, Elizabeth, and talk   1070
Of friends who suffer in the torn
Old Europe where we both were born,
What this refutes or that confirms,
I can but think our talk in terms

Of images that I have seen,
And England tells me what we mean.
Thus, squalid beery BURTON stands
For shoddy thinking of all brands;
The wreck of RHONDDA for the mess
We make when for a short success   1080
We split our symmetry apart,
Deny the Reason or the Heart;
YE OLDE TUDOR TEA-SHOPPE for
The folly of dogmatic law,
While graceless BOURNEMOUTH is the sloth
Of men or bureaucrats or both.

No matter where, or whom I meet,
Shop-gazing in a Paris street,
Bumping through Iceland in a bus,
At teas when clubwomen discuss   1090
The latest Federation Plan,
In Pullman washrooms, man to man,
Hearing how circumstance has vexed
A broker who is oversexed,
In houses where they do not drink,
Whenever I begin to think
About the human creature we
Must nurse to sense and decency,
An English area comes to mind,
I see the nature of my kind   1100
As a locality I love,
Those limestone moors that stretch from BROUGH
To HEXHAM and the ROMAN WALL,
There is my symbol of us all.
There, where the EDEN leisures through

Its sandstone valley, is my view
Of green and civil life that dwells
Below a cliff of savage fells
From which original address
Man faulted into consciousness.   1110
Along the line of lapse the fire
Of life's impersonal desire
Burst through his sedentary rock
And, as at DUFTON and at KNOCK,
Thrust up between his mind and heart
Enormous cones of myth and art.
Always my boy of wish returns
To those peat-stained deserted burns
That feed the WEAR and TYNE and TEES,
And, turning states to strata, sees   1120
How basalt long oppressed broke out
In wild revolt at CAULDRON SNOUT,
And from the relics of old mines
Derives his algebraic signs
For all in man that mourns and seeks,
For all of his renounced techniques,
Their tramways overgrown with grass,
For lost belief, for all Alas,
The derelict lead-smelting mill,
Flued to its chimney up the hill,   1130
That smokes no answer any more
But points, a landmark on BOLTS LAW,
The finger of all questions. There
In ROOKHOPE I was first aware
Of Self and Not-self, Death and Dread:
Adits were entrances which led
Down to the Outlawed, to the Others,

The Terrible, the Merciful, the Mothers;
Alone in the hot day I knelt
Upon the edge of shafts and felt   1140
The deep *Urmutterfurcht* that drives
Us into knowledge all our lives,
The far interior of our fate
To civilize and to create,
Das Weibliche that bids us come
To find what we're escaping from.
There I dropped pebbles, listened, heard
The reservoir of darkness stirred;
'*O deine Mutter kehrt dir nicht*
Wieder. Du selbst bin ich, dein' Pflicht   1150
Und Liebe. Brach sie nun mein Bild."
And I was conscious of my guilt.

But such a bond is not an Ought,
Only a given mode of thought,
Whence my imperatives were taught.
Now in that other world I stand
Of fully alienated land,
An earth made common by the means
Of hunger, money, and machines,
Where each determined nature must   1160
Regard that nature as a trust
That, being chosen, he must choose,
Determined to become of use;
For we are conscripts to our age
Simply by being born; we wage
The war we are, and may not die
With POLYCARP's despairing cry,
Desert or become ill: but how

To be the patriots of the Now?
Then all, by rights, are volunteers,   1170
And anyone who interferes
With how another wills to fight
Must base his action, not on right,
But on the power to compel.
Only the 'Idiot' can tell
For which state office he should run,
Only the Many make the One.

Eccentric, wrinkled, and ice-capped,
Swarming with parasites and wrapped
In a peculiar atmosphere,   1180
Earth wabbles on down her career
With no ambition in her heart;
Her loose land-masses drift apart,
Her zone of shade and silence crawls
Steadily westward. Daylight falls
On Europe's frozen soldiery
And millions brave enough to die
For a new day; for each one knows
A day is drawing to a close.
Yes, all of us at least know that,   1190
All from the seasoned diplomat
Used to the warm Victorian summers
Down to the juveniles and drummers.
Whatever nonsense we believe,
Whomever we can still deceive,
Whatever language angers us,
Whoever seems the poisonous
Old dragon to be killed if men
Are ever to be rich again,

We know no fuss or pain or lying
Can stop the moribund from dying,
That all the special tasks begun
By the Renaissance have been done.

When unity has come to grief
Upon professional belief,
Another unity was made
By equal amateurs in trade.
Out of the noise and horror, the
Opinions of artillery,
The barracks chatter and the yell   1210
Of charging cavalry, the smell
Of poor opponents roasting, out
Of LUTHER's faith and MONTAIGNE's doubt,
The epidemic of translations,
The Councils and the navigations,
The confiscations and the suits,
The scholars' scurrilous disputes
Over the freedom of the Will
And right of Princes to do ill,
Emerged a new *Anthropos,* an   1220
Empiric Economic Man,
The urban, prudent, and inventive,
Profit his rational incentive
And Work his whole *exercitus,*
The individual let loose
To guard himself, at liberty
To starve or be forgotten, free
To feel in splendid isolation
Or drive himself about creation
In the closed cab of Occupation.   1230

55

He did what he was born to do,
Proved some assumptions were untrue.
He had his half-success; he broke
The silly and unnatural yoke
Of famine and disease that made
A false necessity obeyed;
A Protestant, he found the key
To Catholic economy,
Subjected earth to the control
And moral choices of the soul;   1240
And in the training of each sense
To serve with joy its evidence
He founded a new discipline
To fight an intellectual sin,
Reason's depravity that takes
The useful concepts that she makes
As universals, as the *kitsch,*
But worshiped statues upon which
She leaves her effort and her crown,
And if his half-success broke down,   1250
All failures have one good result:
They prove the Good is difficult.

He never won complete support;
However many votes he bought.
He could not silence all the cliques,
And no miraculous techniques
Could sterilize all discontent
Or dazzle it into assent,
But at the very noon and arch
Of his immense triumphal march   1260
Stood prophets pelting him with curses

And sermons and satiric verses,
And ostentatious beggars slept.
BLAKE shouted insults, ROUSSEAU wept,
Ironic KIERKEGAARD stared long
And muttered 'All are in the wrong,'
While BAUDELAIRE went mad protesting
That progress is not interesting
And thought he was an albatross,
The great Erotic on the cross   1270
Of Science, crucified by fools
Who sit all day on office stools,
Are fairly faithful to their wives
And play for safety all their lives,
For whose *Verbürgerlichung* of
All joy and suffering and love
Let the grand pariah atone
By dying hated and alone.

The World ignored them; they were few.
The careless victor never knew   1280
Their grapevine rumor would grow true,
Their alphabet of warning sounds
The common grammar all have grounds
To study; for their guess is proved:
It is the Mover that is moved.
Whichever way we turn, we see
Man captured by his liberty,
The measurable taking charge
Of him who measures, set at large
By his own actions, useful facts   1290
Become the user of his acts,
And Chance the choices of his soul;

The beggar put out by his bowl,
Boys trained by factories for leading
Unusual lives as nurses, feeding
Helpless machines, girls married off
To typewriters, old men in love
With prices they can never get,
Homes blackmailed by a radio set,
Children inherited by slums   1300
And idiots by enormous sums:
We see, we suffer, we despair.
The well-armed children everywhere
Who envy the self-governed beast
Now know that they are bound at least,
Die Aufgeregten without pity
Destroying the historic city,
The ruined showering with honors
The blind Christs and the mad Madonnas,
The Gnostics in the brothels treating   1310
The flesh as secular and fleeting,
The *dialegesthai* of the rich
At cocktail parties as to which
Technique is most effective in
Enforcing labor discipline,
What Persian Apparatus will
Protect their privileges still
And safely keep the living dead
Entombed, hilarious, and fed,
The Disregarded in their shacks   1320
Upon the wrong side of the tracks,
Poisoned by reasonable hate,
Are symptoms of one common fate.
All in their morning mirrors face

A member of a governed race.
Each recognizes what LEAR saw,
The *homo* THURBER likes to draw,
The neuter outline that's the plan
And icon of Industrial Man,
The Unpolitical afraid   1330
Of all that has to be obeyed.

But still each private citizen
Thanks God he's not as other men.
O all too easily we blame
The politicians for our shame
And the hired officers of state
For all those customs that frustrate
Our own intention to fulfill
Eros's legislative will.
Yet who must not, if he reflect,   1340
See how unserious the effect
That he to love's volition gives,
On what base compromise he lives?
Even true lovers on some bed
The graceful God has visited
Find faults at which to hang the head,
And know the morphon full of guilt
Whence all community is built,
The cryptozoön with two backs
Whose sensibility that lacks   1350
True reverence contributes much
Towards the soldier's violent touch.
For, craving language and a myth
And hands to shape their purpose with,
In shadow round the fond and warm

59

The possible societies swarm,
Because their freedom as their form
Upon our sense of style depends,
Whose eyes alone can seek their ends,
And they are impotent if we   1360
Decline responsibility.
O what can love's intention do
If all his agents are untrue?
The politicians we condemn
Are nothing but our L. C. M.
The average of the average man
Becomes the dread Leviathan,
Our million individual deeds,
Omissions, vanities, and creeds,
Put through the statistician's hoop   1370
The gross behavior of a group.
Upon each English conscience lie
Two decades of hypocrisy,
And not a German can be proud
Of what his apathy allowed.

The flood of tyranny and force
Arises at a double source:
In PLATO's lie of intellect
That all are weak but the Elect
Philosophers who must be strong,   1380
For, knowing Good, they will no Wrong,
United in the abstract Word
Above the low anarchic herd;
Or ROUSSEAU's falsehood of the flesh
That stimulates our pride afresh
To think all men identical

And strong in the Irrational.
And yet, although the social lie
Looks double to the dreamer's eye,
The rain to fill the mountain streams 1390
That water the opposing dreams
By turns in favor with the crowd
Is scattered from one common cloud.
Up in the Ego's atmosphere
And higher altitudes of fear
The particles of error form
The shepherd-killing thunderstorm,
And our political distress
Descends from her self-consciousness,
Her cold *concupiscence d'esprit* 1400
That looks upon her liberty
Not as a gift from life with which
To serve, enlighten, and enrich
The total creature that could use
Her function of free-will to choose
The actions that this world requires
To educate its blind desires,
But as the right to lead alone
An attic life all on her own,
Unhindered, unrebuked, unwatched, 1410
Self-known, self-praising, self-attached.
All happens as she wishes till
She ask herself why she should will
This more than that, or who would care
If she were dead or gone elsewhere,
And on her own hypothesis
Is powerless to answer this.
Then panic seizes her; the glance

61

Of mirrors shows a countenance
Of wretched empty-brilliance. How   1420
Can she escape self-loathing now?
What is there left for pride to do
Except plunge headlong *vers la boue,*
For freedom except suicide,
The self-asserted, self-denied?
A witch self-tortured as she spins
Her whole devotion widdershins,
She worships in obscene delight
The Not, the Never, and the Night,
The formless Mass without a Me,   1430
The Midnight Women and the Sea.
The genius of the loud Steam Age,
Loud WAGNER, put it on the stage:
The mental hero who has swooned
With sensual pleasure at his wound,
His intellectual life fulfilled
In knowing that his doom is willed,
Exists to suffer; borne along
Upon a timeless tide of song,
The huge doll roars for death or mother, 1440
Synonymous with one another;
And Woman, passive as in dreams,
Redeems, redeems, redeems, redeems.

Delighted with their takings, bars
Are closing under fading stars;
The revelers go home to change
Back into something far more strange,
The tightened self in which they may
Walk safely through their bothered day,

With formal purpose up and down   1450
The crowded fatalistic town,
And dawn sheds its calm candor now
On monasteries where they vow
An economic abstinence.
Modern in their impenitence,
Blonde, naked, paralyzed, alone,
Like rebel angels turned to stone
The secular cathedrals stand
Upon their valuable land,
Frozen forever in a lie,   1460
Determined always to deny
That man is weak and has to die,
And hide the huge phenomena
Which must decide America,
That culture that had worshiped no
Virgin before the Dynamo,
Held no Nicea nor Canossa,
Hat keine verfallenen Schlösser,
Keine Basalte, the great Rome
To all who lost or hated home.   1470

A long time since it seems today
The Saints in Massachusetts Bay
Heard theocratic COTTON preach
And legal WINTHROP's Little Speech;
Since MISTRESS HUTCHINSON was tried
By those her Inner Light defied,
And WILLIAMS questioned Moses' law
But in Rhode Island waited for
The Voice of the Beloved to free
Himself and the Democracy;   1480

63

Long since inventive JEFFERSON
Fought realistic HAMILTON,
Pelagian versus Jansenist;
But the same heresies exist.
Time makes old formulas look strange,
Our properties and symbols change,
But round the freedom of the Will
Our disagreements centre still,
And now as then the voter hears
The battle cries of two ideas.   1490
Here, as in Europe, is dissent,
This raw untidy continent
Where the Commuter can't forget
The Pioneer; and even yet
A *Völkerwanderung* occurs:
Resourceful manufacturers
Trek southward by progressive stages
For sites with no floor under wages,
No ceiling over hours; and by
Artistic souls in towns that lie   1500
Out in the weed and pollen belt
The need for sympathy is felt,
And east to hard New York they come;
And self-respect drives Negroes from
The one-crop and race-hating delta
To northern cities helter-skelter;
And in jalopies there migrates
A rootless tribe from windblown states
To suffer further westward where
The tolerant Pacific air   1510
Makes logic seem so silly, pain
Subjective, what he seeks so vain

The wanderer may die; and kids,
When their imagination bids,
Hitch-hike a thousand miles to find
The Hesperides that's on their mind,
Some Texas where real cowboys seem
Lost in a movie-cowboy's dream.
More even than in Europe, here
The choice of patterns is made clear   1520
Which the machine imposes, what
Is possible and what is not,
To what conditions we must bow
In building the Just City now.

However we decide to act,
Decision must accept the fact
That the machine has now destroyed
The local customs we enjoyed,
Replaced the bonds of blood and nation
By personal confederation.   1530
No longer can we learn our good
From chances of a neighborhood
Or class or party, or refuse
As individuals to choose
Our loves, authorities, and friends,
To judge our means and plan our ends;
For the machine has cried aloud
And publicized among the crowd
The secret that was always true
But known once only to the few,   1540
Compelling all to the admission,
Aloneness is man's real condition,
That each must travel forth alone

In search of the Essential Stone,
'The Nowhere-without-No' that is
The justice of societies.
Each salesman now is the polite
Adventurer, the landless knight
GAWAINE-QUIXOTE, and his goal
The *Frauendienst* of his weak soul;   1550
Each biggie in the Canning Ring
An unrobust lone FISHER-KING;
Each subway face the PEQUOD of
Some ISHMAEL hunting his lost love,
To harpoon his unhappiness
And turn the whale to a princess;
In labs the puzzled KAFKAS meet
The inexplicable defeat:
The odd behavior of the law,
The facts that suddenly withdraw,   1560
The path that twists away from the
Near-distant CASTLE they can see,
The Truth where they will be denied
Permission ever to reside;
And all the operatives know
Their factory is the *champ-clos*
And drawing-room of HENRY JAMES,
Where the *débat* decides the claims
Of liberty and justice; where,
Like any Jamesian character,   1570
They learn to draw the careful line,
Develop, understand, refine.

A weary Asia out of sight
Is tugging gently at the night,

Uncovering a restless race;
Clocks shoo the childhood from its face,
And accurate machines begin
To concentrate its adults in
A narrow day to exercise
Their gifts in some cramped enterprise.   1580
How few pretend to like it: O
Three quarters of these people know
Instinctively what ought to be
The nature of society
And how they'd live there if they could.
If it were easy to be good,
And cheap, and plain as evil how,
We all would be its members now.
How readily would we become
The seamless live continuum   1590
Of supple and coherent stuff,
Whose form is truth, whose content love,
Its pluralistic interstices
The homes of happiness and peace,
Where in a unity of praise
The largest *publicum's* a *res,*
And the least *res* a *publicum;*
How grandly would our virtues bloom
In a more conscionable dust
Where Freedom dwells because it must,   1600
Necessity because it can,
And men confederate in Man.

But wishes are not horses, this
Annus is not *mirabilis;*
Day breaks upon the world we know

Of war and wastefulness and woe;
Ashamed civilians come to grief
In brotherhoods without belief,
Whose good intentions cannot cure
The actual evils they endure, 1610
Nor smooth their practical career,
Nor bring the far horizon near.
The New Year brings an earth afraid,
Democracy a ready-made
And noisy tradesman's slogan, and
The poor betrayed into the hand
Of lackeys with ideas, and truth
Whipped by their elders out of youth,
The peaceful fainting in their tracks
With martyrs' tombstones on their backs, 1620
And culture on all fours to greet
A butch and criminal élite,
While in the vale of silly sheep
Rheumatic old patricians weep.

Our news is seldom good: the heart,
As ZOLA said, must always start
The day by swallowing its toad
Of failure and disgust. Our road
Gets worse and we seem altogether
Lost as our theories, like the weather, 1630
Veer round completely every day,
And all that we can always say
Is: true democracy begins
With free confession of our sins.
In this alone are all the same,
All are so weak that none dare claim

68

'I have the right to govern,' or
'Behold in me the Moral Law,'
And all real unity commences
In consciousness of differences,   1640
That all have needs to satisfy
And each a power to supply.
We need to love all since we are
Each a unique particular
That is no giant, god, or dwarf,
But one odd human isomorph;
We can love each because we know
All, all of us, that this is so:
Can live because we've lived, the powers
That we create with are not ours.   1650

O Unicorn among the cedars,
To whom no magic charm can lead us,
White childhood moving like a sigh
Through the green woods unharmed in thy
Sophisticated innocence,
To call thy true love to the dance,
O Dove of science and of light,
Upon the branches of the night,
O Ichthus playful in the deep
Sea-lodges that forever keep   1660
Their secret of excitement hidden,
O sudden Wind that blows unbidden,
Parting the quiet reeds, O Voice
Within the labyrinth of choice
Only the passive listener hears,
O Clock and Keeper of the years,
O Source of equity and rest,

Quando non fuerit, non est,
It without image, paradigm
Of matter, motion, number, time,   1670
The grinning gap of Hell, the hill
Of Venus and the stairs of Will,
Disturb our negligence and chill,
Convict our pride of its offence
In all things, even penitence,
Instruct us in the civil art
Of making from the muddled heart
A desert and a city where
The thoughts that have to labor there
May find locality and peace,   1680
And pent-up feelings their release,
Send strength sufficient for our day,
And point our knowledge on its way,
O da quod jubes, Domine.

Dear friend Elizabeth, dear friend
These days have brought me, may the end
I bring to the grave's dead-line be
More worthy of your sympathy
Than the beginning; may the truth
That no one marries lead my youth   1690
Where you already are and bless
Me with your learned peacefulness,
Who on the lives about you throw
A calm *solificatio,*
A warmth throughout the universe
That each for better or for worse
Must carry round with him through life,
A judge, a landscape, and a wife.

We fall down in the dance, we make
The old ridiculous mistake,   1700
But always there are such as you
Forgiving, helping what we do.
O every day in sleep and labor
Our life and death are with our neighbor,
And love illuminates again
The city and the lion's den,
The world's great rage, the travel of young men.

NOTES

PART I

13 *The same wishful-thinking sigh*

Clocks cannot tell our time of day
For what event to pray
Because we have no time, because
We have no time until
We know what time we fill,
Why time is other than time was.

Nor can our question satisfy
The answer in the statue's eye:
Only the living ask whose brow
May wear the Roman laurel now;
The dead say only how.

What happens to the living when we die?
Death is not understood by Death; nor You, nor I.

30 *Yet Time can moderate his tone*

In his *Reminiscences of Tolstoi,* Maxim Gorki tells
how he came one day unobserved upon the great man
who was attentively regarding a lizard sunning itself
on a stone. "Are you happy?" Tolstoi asked the lizard.
Then, after looking round to make sure that no one
was watching, he said confidentially: "I'm not."

75

"The German team won the world chess champion-
ship last night, beating the Polish team by one half
point."

Despatch from Buenos Aires. Sept 19, 1939.

*   *   *

On the other hand, the private incident may seem
all too symbolic. M tells me that, on the day war was
declared, her Scotch terrier was playing with her neigh-
bour's small kitten, and played so roughly that he
broke its skull.

56 *To set in order*

"O Thou who lovest me, set my love in order"
Jacopone da Todi
(quoted by E. M. Forster in *What I Believe*)

60 *That order which must be the end*
That all self-loving things intend

>   Every man adopts to food
>   A scientific attitude,
>   When he wants to kiss his wife
>   Leads a politician's life,
>   And, so far as it is known,
>   Is an artist when alone.

62 *Who struggle for their liberty*

The concept of freedom presupposes the existence of
a composite group and is concerned with the relations
of the different members of that group to each other
and to the whole which they collectively form, and

that this relation is a two-way relation. From the point of view of the whole, of internal relations, freedom means unity, the harmonious agreement of the parts; from the point of view of each of the parts, of external relations, freedom means the right of that part to realise to the full its potential nature without interference from the others. Treat all relations as internal and to be free comes to mean to be homogeneous, i.e., to have abolished all external relations (Pantheism). Treat all relations as external and to be free comes to mean to be the only existence in the universe, i.e., to have abolished internal relations (Solipsism). Further, freedom is a concept of conscious human beings, and is, as Engels defines it, a consciousness of necessity. Just as there are two aspects of freedom, there are, humanely speaking, two aspects of necessity, the causal and the logical. Causal necessity (Fortune) decrees what shall be presented to consciousness from the outside through the sense organs, or through memory, as images from the unconscious. Logical necessity (Virtue) governs everything once it has reached consciousness (a thing cannot simultaneously be A and Not-A).

Fundamentally, however, one could define consciousness as the capacity to be modified by experience, i.e., a thing is conscious to the degree that events leave traces in it, after they have ceased to happen, so that in this sense absolute unconsciousness does not exist and all things show *some* degree of logic in their behavior (hence the statistical nature of physical laws). To say that one thing was more conscious than another would then be to say that it is modified by a greater number and variety of events.

When we say that we have free-will, we want to be saying that the number and variety of events by which we are modified are so great that for us the process of learning is continuous; *every* moment events occur which add their traces to the traces left by past events and modify them, so that what seems to us necessary, changes from moment to moment. In consequence the *Now* we must accept, our freedom *to,* is continually changing into the *Then* we must reject, our freedom *from.* Choice is our term for expressing the continuity of this change. But there is no escape from necessity. A dictatorship has been defined as a state where everything that is not forbidden is obligatory. In that sense, human beings have always lived under a dictatorship and always will.

78 *Art is not life and cannot be*
   A midwife to society

"You may say, 'But what about politics? What about the interests of the state?' But great writers engage in politics only in so far as it is necessary to defend people against politics. The role of Paul is more fitting to a writer than of Saul."

Anton Tchekov. *Letter to A. S. Souvorin*

*　　　*　　　*

Both their unique position in society and the unique nature of their work conspire to make artists less fitted for political thinking than most people. As citizens they are the *only* people for whom a capitalist democracy is a completely open society. Despite every publisher's trick the relation between an artist and the public is one to which *laissez-faire* economics really applies, for there is neither coercion nor competition. In consequence the successful artist (the one on good terms with society), thinking that what is sauce for the goose is sauce for the gander, is an anarchist at heart who, like a peasant proprietor, hates *all* government for whose interference he has no personal cause to see the necessity. Who has ever met a left-wing intellectual (at least one who has had any success) for whom the real attraction of Communism did not lie in its promise that, under it, the state should wither away for others as it has already withered away for him?

But what of the more embittered type of artist, embittered either from failure in his personal life or because his work is not appreciated, who is therefore on bad terms with society? His political thinking cannot be based on an objective view of society from his unique social position *qua* artist—for, in so far as he is unsuccessful, he is, socially speaking, no artist at all, but just a failure, along with all the other failures, with the unemployed, tramps, footpads and prostitutes whom society does not recognize. No, it can be only based upon introspective observation of his own activity, i.e., of the artistic creative process. Now, just as the artist *qua* citizen is the only person for whom society is really open, so, *qua* artist, i.e., in relation to what he does, he is the only person who is really a dictator. Works of art really are closed societies, and they are made (except for drama and architecture) by the artist alone without any social assistance. Political generalizations, based on the introspection of artists, will tend therefore to be "idealist" and anti-democratic, (e.g. *The Plumed Serpent*). It is not surprising that Hitler began as a painter and has derived such inspiration from Wagner (see 1443). All anti-intellectual Blood-and-Soil ideologies bear the marks of their origin among unsuccessful intellectuals: Utopias planned by artists *manqués* over café tables very late at night.

83 . . . *it presents*
Already lived experience
Through a convention that creates
Autonomous completed states

"The problem of 'wholeness' is connected in different ways with the process of induction, as with most other processes of early development. A small piece of the upper blastopore lip can induce a whole embryo, a little fragment of the archenteric root, a whole medullary plate. In doing so, the inductors, in part, regulate themselves to a whole, out of their own material in advance, in part, they complete themselves out of the adjacent material. If a piece of totipotent ectoderm is implanted into the epidermis of another germ, it does not form part of the new surroundings according to the needs of the new place, but gives origin to the most different organs, in accordance with the region of the germ. Thus here, too, the induced formation approaches that of a whole. Still more remarkable are the results of heteroplastic and xenoplastic induction. They can only be explained by the assumption that they are 'ordered,' as it were, as a whole. . . . The larva of *Triton* has genuine teeth in its mouth, of the same structure and origin as the teeth of all verte-brates; the mouth of the tadpole, on the other hand, is furnished with horny jaws and have stumps which are very different in origin and structure from genuine teeth and probably without any morphological relation to them. . . .

"Horny jaws have been induced in the mouthfield of *Triton*, with all desirable evidence by O. Schotte. In one case, where the implant covered the whole mouth region, the typical mouth of a tadpole was developed into the normal half-mouth of a *Triton* with genuine teeth. Holtfreter has in the meantime also obtained the same formations in great number and perfection, likewise in the reciprocal experiment, genuine teeth from transplanted urodele ectoderm in anuran larva. . . . It is not surprising that head organs are induced in the head field, nor that these organs possess the structure which corresponds to the store of potencies in the frog-skin, but it is surprising that anything is induced at all. It is new and surprising that the potencies of the frog ectoderm respond to the inductive stimulus of the *Triton* head, that is, that potencies for organs which *Triton* does not possess at all, respond to stimuli which normally release quite different formations. . . . We may already assert with confidence concerning the nature of the inducing stimulus that it must be very specialized as to what is to be formed, but quite indifferent as to how it is to be formed. It is as if the 'cue' were only quite general. 'Mouth Armament,' and at this cue the needed organs would be formed as they are provided in the genotype of the reacting tissue."

Hans Spemann.
Embryonic Development and Induction.

81

"The germ, wherever gathered, has ever been for me the germ of a 'story,' and most of the stories straining to shape under my hand have sprung from a single small seed, a seed as minute and minute as that casual hint for 'The Spoils of Poynton' dropped unwittingly by my neighbor, a mere floating particle in the stream of talk. What above all comes back to me with this reminiscence is the sense of the inveterate minuteness, on such happy occasions, of the precious particle—reduced, that is, to its mere fruitful essence. Such is the interesting truth about the stray suggestion, the wandering word, the vague echo, at touch of which the novelist's imagination winces as at the prick of some sharp point: its virtue is all in its needle-like quality, the power to penetrate as finely as possible. This fineness it is that communicates the virus of suggestion, anything more than the minimum of which spoils the operation. . . . It at the same time amuses him (the artist) again and again to note how, beyond the first step of the actual case, the case that constitutes for him his germ, his vital particle, his grain of gold, life persistently blunders and deviates, loses herself in the sand. The reason is of course that life has no direct sense whatever for the subject and is capable, luckily for us, of nothing but splendid waste. . . . If life in presenting us the germ, and left merely to herself in such a business, gives the case away, almost always, before we can stop her, what are the signs for our guidance, what the primary laws for a saving selection, how do we know when and where to intervene, where do we place the beginnings of the wrong or right deviation? Such would be the elements of an inquiry upon which, I hasten to say, it is quite forbidden me here to embark: I but glance at them in evidence of the rich pasture that at every turn surrounds the ruminant critic."

Henry James.
Preface to The Spoils of Poynton.

*   *   *

Motionless, deep in his mind lies the past the poet's
    forgotten,
Till some small experience wake it to life and a poem's
    begotten,
Words its presumptive primordia, Feeling its field of
    induction,
Meaning its pattern of growth determined during
    construction.

87 *Though their particulars are those*
   That each particular artist knows

> Who managed in the Spanish War
> Not only to write well but be
> Of some use to the military?
> Was it not the three or four
> Lonely specialists in whose
> Soul and body learning why
> People kill and how they die,
> The ethics of defeat, the sense
> Of sanctity in violence,
> Aroused as genuine pleasure as
> That complex desolation which
> Made Proust go slumming all his life
> Among the idle and the rich,
> Or those awkward daughters of

The country vicar's worried life
Upon whose sly ambition once
Jane Austen with a kind of love
Sharpened her intelligence?

108 *social unsuccess*

"If we generalize human relations too much, demand
too little of them, we will lose the sense of gaps and
deficiencies which set some children to dreaming. . . .
The child is not born wanting a father, he is taught
his need by the social blessedness of others. No Samoan
child, in a society where the parent child relationship
is diffused over dozens of adults, would dream of creat-
ing an ideal father; nor do the Samoans, finding such
quiet satisfaction among their uncritical equals, build
a heaven which reverberates on earth. Neither does
the Manus child or adult build pictures of the ideal
wife or mother, for his society does not suggest to him
that it would be possible to find one. If we substitute
for father-to-child relationships, only contacts with
adults of the opposite sex and the applause of the age
group, if we erect standards of casual relationships be-
tween the sexes, relationships without strength or re-
sponsibility, we have no guarantee of so stimulating
individuals to use imaginatively in new ways the rich
and diverse materials of our cultural inheritance."

Margaret Meade. *Growing up in New Guinea.*

109 *Hunted you out of life*

"A man cannot in reason embark upon 'the volun-
tary' (the requirements of which are higher than the

universal requirements) unless he has an *immediate* certainty that it is required of him *in particular*. From the point of view of the universal requirements, 'the voluntary' is in fact presumption; and consequently one must have immediate certainty that the particular is required of one in order to be able to embark upon it. . . . In order really to be a great genius, a man must be an exception. But in order that his being exceptional should be a serious matter he himself must be unfree, forced into the position. There lies the importance of his dementia. There is a definite point in which he suffers; it is impossible for him to run with the herd. Perhaps his dementia has nothing whatsoever to do with his real genius, but it is the pain by which he is nailed out in isolation—and he must be isolated if he is to be great; and no man can freely isolate himself; he must be compelled if it is to be a serious matter."

Journals of Soren Kierkegaard.

*   *   *

Definition of aesthetics   The rules of a game.

Definition of a game   Any action or series of actions that can be done perfectly.

Definition of Art   The most difficult game conceivable to man.

And what is the only thing that can never become a game, but always remains work, i.e., which can never be done perfectly and so give us aesthetic satisfaction? *The ethical.*

Definition of a classical artist   One whose dementia is simply the occasion of release for his talent.

Definition of a romantic artist   One whose dementia becomes his subject matter.

Definition of a saint   One to whom ethics have almost become aesthetics.

Definition of God   He to whom everything is child's play.

The moral mania (Tolstoi)   To imagine that man can play at ethics, that art is not a conjuring trick, but magic, that Mrs. Beecher Stowe was God.

The aesthetic mania (Pater)   To imagine that because art cannot assimilate ethics, therefore ethics do not exist, that God is a child.

The psychological mania (Freud)   To imagine that all search for perfection is work, a neurotic refusal to play the game of "normality" (the search for heaven, power and the love of women), that God-O.

Definition of an artist   One whose desire for ethical perfection is *exactly* balanced by his cowardice, his fear of what the attempt to achieve perfection will involve. (It is possible that an artistic talent *always* appears where this equilibrium obtains and *only* then.) Were his talent a fraction greater, he would certainly become a madman or a crook; were it a fraction less, he would probably be compelled to attempt to become a saint.

A poet's prayer   "Lord, teach me to write so well, that I shall no longer want to."

111 *Yet the live quarry all the same*
Were changed to huntsmen in the game

"Do, please, write a story of how a young man, the son of a serf, who has been a shopboy, a chorister, pupil of

86

a secondary school and a university graduate, who had been brought up to respect rank and to kiss the priest's hand, to bow to other people's ideas, to be thankful for each morsel of bread, who has been thrashed many a time, who has had to walk about tutoring without galoshes, who has fought, tormented animals, has been fond of dining at the house of well-to-do relations, and played the hypocrite both to God and man without any need but merely out of consciousness of his own insignificance, describe how that young man squeezes the slave out of himself, drop by drop, and how, awakening one fine morning, he feels running in his veins no longer the blood of a slave but genuine human blood."

Anton Tchekov. *Letter to A. S. Souvorin.*

130 *The greatest of vocations chose*

Few the vocations that conform to Society's ethos,
And lucky those they select, their happiness ready
    made.

     *   *   *

—"Doctor or Hangman, which shall I be? Both need
    similar gifts—"
—"Don't worry, dear: I am sure you'll be of use to the
    town—"

     *   *   *

Parents once upon a time
Thought that acting was a crime;
"Daughter," many of them said,
"We would rather see you dead
Than upon a public stage."
Ours is a more liberal age:
Not a father breaks his heart

87

If she does Commercial Art,
Not a mother's hair turns grey
If her only son to-day
Find an outlet of expression
In the journalist profession.

142 *That summary tribunal*

"Only our concept of Time makes it possible for us
to speak of the Day of Judgment by that name; in
reality it is a summary court in perpetual session."

Franz Kafka. Aphorisms.

195 *Muttering that terror is not French*

"Allons! La marche, le fardeau, le désert, l'ennui et
la colère. A qui me louer? Quelle bête faut-il adorer?
Quel sainte image attaque-t-on? Quels coeurs briserai-
je? Quel mensonge dois-je tenir?— Dans quel sang
marcher?"

Plutôt, se garder de la justice—La vie dure, l'abru-
tissement simple,—soulever, le poing desséché, le cou-
vercle du cercueil, s'asseoir, s'étouffer. Ainsi point de
viellesse, ni de dangers: la terreur n'est past francaise."

Rimbaud. Une Saison en Enfer.

215 *And Rilke whom die Dinge bless.*

"This small forgotten object that is ready to signify
everything, made you intimate with thousands through
playing a thousand parts, being animal and tree and
king and child—and when it withdrew, they were all
there. This Something, worthless as it was, prepared

your relationships with the world, it guided you into happening, and among people, and, further; you experienced through it, through its existence, its anyhow appearance, through its final smashing or its enigmatic departure, all that is human, right into the depths of death."

R. M. Rilke. *Dolls*

220 *With slip and slapdash what I do*

As Cyril Connolly has pointed out in his brilliant book *Enemies of Promise,* the characteristic vice of the writer to-day is overproduction, and the major cause of overproduction is a need for money. Failing a private income or a complaisant patron, he must either take some non-literary employment and write in his spare time or reduce his standard of living. The conditions of modern employment, however, are such, that really his only choice lies between overproduction and living very simply indeed.

224 *Not to sell cheap what is most dear*

Alas, 'tis true I have gone here and there
And made myself a motley to the view,
Gor'd mine own thoughts, sold cheap what is most dear,
Made old offences of affections new.

Shakespeare. *Sonnet CX*

226 *One instant's toil to Thee denied*
  Stands all eternity's offence
    v. Rudyard Kipling. *My New-Cut Ashlar.*

231 *the sin*
  Peculiar to his discipline

Isolation. The Ivory Tower.
What do they mean, these catchwords of the hour?
Of course every man is alone in his gift
Round which the endless clouds of error drift.
To stand on the top of his talent and make out
More and more of the landscape round about
Is a job that is more than sufficient to tax him:
Something of Everything is a rotten maxim.

275 *The Jew wrecked in the German cell*

How he survived them they could never understand:
Had they not beggared him themselves to prove
They could not live without their dogmas or their
      land?

No worlds they drove him from were ever big enough:
How *could* it be the earth the Unconfined
Meant when It bade them set no limits to their love?

And he fulfilled the rôle for which he was designed:
On heat with fear, he drew their terrors to him,
And was a godsend to the lowest of mankind.

Till there was no place left where they could still
      pursue him
Except that exile which he called his Race.
But, envying him even that, they plunged right
      through him

Into a land of mirrors without time or space,
And all they had to strike now was the human face.

"The Greeks felt that arête was, above everything else, a power, an ability to do something. Strength and health are the arête of the body; cleverness and insight the arête of the mind. The word must originally have been an objective description of the worth of its possession. It means a power which is peculiar to himself, which makes him a complete man."
                                        Werner Jaeger. *Paideia.*

*   *   *

X was a Prussian Junker. Ruined by the Post-War inflation, he took a job as private detective in a Berlin department store. He had not been there long before he had to arrest his own grandmother for shoplifting.

280 *His thoughts towards the Minotaur*
    To take an early boat for Crete

"Ah, this old Minotaur. What he has already cost us. Every year all Europe strikes up the cry: 'Off to Crete. Off to Crete.' "
                Nietzsche. Postscript to *The Case of Wagner.*

*   *   *
                    Nietzsche
O masterly debunker of our liberal fallacies, how
Well you flayed each low Utilitarian and
All the arid prudence of their so-called Rational Man
That made envy the one basis of all moral acts.

All your life you stormed, like your English fore-
        runner Blake,
Warning, Nietzsche, against that decadent tradition

Which in Luther appeared a fragrant and promising
    bloom:
Soon Europe swarmed with your clerical followers.

In dim Victorian days you prophesied a reaction,
And how right you've been. But tell us, O tell us, is
This tenement gangster with a sub-machine gun in
    one hand

Really the Superman your jealous eyes imagined,
That dark Daemonic One whose voice would cleave
    the rock open
And offer our moribund era the water of life?

283 *silly, at its feet*

During the last war Frau M was in Tübingen. Walk-
ing home one cloudy night, she met two professors
from the university, carrying rifles.
    "What's the matter?" she asked.
    "There's an enemy aeroplane overhead. Can't you
see its pilot-light?"
    "But that's not an aeroplane. That's Jupiter."

PART II

343 *Learn who and where and how we are*

Strolling through the jungle one day, the elephant caught sight of the monkey sitting high up in a tree. "You miserable little creature," he cried. "Look at you, cowering up there. No ambition. No determination. Now look at me. I am so big that when I move a step the whole earth trembles. I am so strong that I can pluck up a tree by the roots at a single tug of my trunk. All the beasts of the jungle admire me. What's the matter with you? Why aren't you like me?" The monkey paused for a moment to catch a flea. "I was sick."

        *   *   *

His aging nature is the same
As when childhood wore its name
In an atmosphere of love
And to itself appeared enough:
Only now when he has come
In walking distance of his tomb,
He at last discovers who
He had always been to whom
He so often was untrue.

344 *The children of a modest star*

"Invertebrates embody the secular value of values in the proterozoic era, reptiles in the mesozoic, and anthropoids only in those later periods which have been categorized as the pleiocene, the pleistocene, and the obscene. Man is not as such the source of value, but the chief embodiment of value is, during the human periods named, to be found somewhere among men."

F. L. Wells. *Values in Social Psychology.*

349 *How hard to stretch imagination*
To live according to our station

"You have only one defect. Your false position, your sorrow, your catarrh of the bowels are all due to it. That is your extraordinary lack of education."

Anton Tchekov. *Letter to His Brother Nicolay.*

353 *Each great I*

"The individual represents only a small part of the hereditary possibilities of its protoplasm, for these include not only the so-called normal, but all the variations possible under experimental as well as so-called normal conditions. The statement that a characteristic is hereditary or determined by heredity and not by environment means merely that it develops within a certain range of environment. . . . The protoplasm which has acquired a persistent gradient has had a definite experience and has learned something, and what it has learned modifies all its later behavior."

C. M. Child. *The Beginnings of*
Unity and Order in Living Things

354 *A process in a process*

"Every object of scientific study is at once a whole within a wider environment to which it has qualitative relations, and a group of parts which have qualitative relations among themselves. Such collections are in continuous change. They are, therefore, things which show process change.

"Process change requires both particle and field theory for its full expression. The properties of space are meaningless apart from the objects associated with that space.

"Ultimately all energy elements used in description must be assumed as different from each other.

"The laws of nature describe statistical regularities and are changing."

Hyman Levy. *Modern Science.*

356 *We are changed by what we change*

Why, dear psychoanalyst,
Are you such a pessimist?
Why, like the old Puritan,
Do you separate in man
Pleasure from Reality?
I might possibly agree
With the first line of your song
—Everything I want is wrong—
But common logic would, I feel,
Conclude from this that sin is real.

362 *Prefer our idées fixes to be*
True of a fixed Reality

> "O wearisome condition of humanity,
> Born under one law and to another bound,
> Vainly begot and yet forbidden vanity,
> Created sick, commanded to be sound."
>
> Fulke Greville. *Mustapha*

384 *The Spirit-that-denies*

Mephistopheles.—*"Ich bin der Geist, der stets verneint."*   Goethe. *Faust.* Part I. Scene 3.

395 *Defending relaxation, he*
Must show impassioned energy

> Der Herr—Des Menschen Tätigkeit kann allzuleicht
> erschlaffen,
> Er liebt sich bald die unbedingte Ruh;
> Drum geb' ich gern ihm den Gesellen zu,
> Der reizt und wirkt und muss als Teufel
> schaffen.
>
> Goethe. *Faust.* Prologue in Heaven.

406 *Diabolus egredietur*
Ante pedes ejus

> v. *Habbakuk.* III, 5.

"The wicked, knowing not God, are but as instruments in the hand of a workman, serving unconsciously, and perishing in the using: the good, on the other hand, serve consciously, and in serving become more perfect."   Spinoza. *Correspondence.*

96

408 *But so much more effective, though*
   Than our well-meaning stupid friends

   Meine Dichterglut war sehr gering
   So lang ich dem Guten entgegen ging;
   Dagegen brannte sie lichterloh
   Wenn ich von drohendem Übel floh.
                    Goethe. *Sprichwörtlich.*

411 *Retro me*
                    v. *St. Matthew.* XVI 23

422 *Credo ut intelligam*
      v. St. Anselm
   To push us into grace

   "It was from out of the rind of an apple tasted that
   the knowledge of good and evil, as two twins cleaving
   together, leaped forth into the world. And perhaps this
   is that doom which Adam fell into of knowing good
   and evil, that is of knowing good by evil."
                    Milton. *Areopagitica.*

447 *Certain patterns in our lives*

   "The problem by which so many have been disturbed
   is indeed no problem at all. This becomes obvious as
   soon as we distinguish between the organism as a
   transphenomenal entity and the 'body' as a percept.
   To the first refers the statement that all percepts de-
   pend on processes inside the organism—where even
   the word *depend,* just as *inside* and *organism,* has a
   transphenomenal meaning. To the second, the 'body-

percept', refers the sentence that things have places 'outside myself'—where all words point to phenomenal facts and 'outside' is a phenomenal relation in phenomenal space. Only if we fail to see that one statement is about relations in transphenomenal space (including the organism) while the other is about relations in phenomenal space (including the 'bodily self')—only so long can we believe that these statements contradict each other. Confuse the organism with the 'self'-percept, fail to distinguish between physical space, and phenomenal space, and you have the great paradox. 'Inside' predicated there contradicts 'outside' found here. I have only to add that the paradox disappears without the help of any special hypothesis. It simply vanishes before consistent thinking on the accepted premises of Epistemological Dualism."

Wolfgang Köhler.
The Place of Value in a World of Facts.

451 *I is not-Elizabeth*

Infants in their mothers' arms
Exercise their budding charms
On their fingers and their toes,
Striving ever to enclose
In the circle of their will
Objects disobedient still.
But the boy comes soon enough
To the limits of self-love,
And the adult learns how small
Is the individual,
How much stronger is the state

That will not co-operate
With the kingdom of his mind:
All his lifetime he will find
Swollen knee or aching tooth
Hostile to his search for truth;
Never will his sex belong
To his world of right and wrong,
Its libido comprehend
Who is foe and who is friend.

497 *l'esprit de géométrie*

"L'esprit a son ordre qui est par principes et demon-
strations; le coeur en a un autre."

Pascal. *Pensées.*

505. *And Chinese wall of Barbara*

He that but once too nearly hears
The music of forefended spheres,
Is thence forth lonely, and for all
His days like one who treads the Wall
Of China, and on his hand sees
Cities and their civilities,
And, on the other, lions.
Coventry Patmore. *The Victories of Love.*

*   *   *

The Devil would, no doubt, stoutly maintain that: "If
a donkey is Plato, it is a great philosopher."

507 *An ordre logique*

W's brother is president of The Artificial Insemina-
tion Society. Every November they hold their annual

picnic. A Moorish temple in tin has been built for the bulls.

508 *O cruel intellect that chills*

According to the statistics given by Dr. Otto Neurath in *Modern Man in the Making,* an increase in the literacy rate has been everywhere (with the exception of the Netherlands) accompanied by an increase in the suicide rate. Again he shows that a weakening of the tyranny of the family is counteracted by an increase in collectivisation, a strengthening of the tyranny of the State.

509 *His natural warmth*

"If by 'natural to children' we mean that a child will learn easily what an adult, culturally defined, and in many ways limited, will not learn except with the greatest difficulty, it is true that any capability upon which the society does not set a premium, will seem easier to teach to a child than to an adult. So our children seem more imaginative than adults because we put a premium upon practical behavior, which is strictly orientated to the world of sense experience. Manus children, on the other hand, seem more practical, more matter-of-fact than do the Manus adults who live in a world where unseen spirits direct many of their activities. An educational enthusiast working among Manus children would be struck with their 'scientific potentialities,' just as the enthusiast among ourselves is struck with our children's 'imaginative potentialities.' The observations in both cases would

be true in relation to the adult culture. In the case of
our children their imaginative tendencies nourished
upon a rich language and varied and diverse literary
tradition will be discounted in adult life, attenuated,
suppressed, distorted by the demands for practical
adjustment; while the Manus children's frank scepti-
cism and preoccupation with what they can see and
touch and hear will be overlaid by the canons of Manus
supernaturalism."

Margaret Meade. *Growing up in New Guinea.*

514 *The hard self-conscious particles*
Collide, divide like numerals

"The life of mankind could very well be conceived as
a speech in which different men represented the vari-
ous parts of speech. . . . How few are substantives,
verbs, etc.: how many are copula . . . There are
people in life whose position is like that of the inter-
jection, without influence in the sentence. They are
the hermits of life and at the very most take a case, e.g.
O me miserum."

Journals of Soren Kierkegaard

516 *And build no order anywhere*

One night in Cuba, being rather drunk, he decided to
get married. He thought of two girls, one of whom he
liked very much, the other not so much. He tele-
graphed a proposal to Number One. She replied that,
if he were serious, he would come home first to see
her. "To hell with her," he thought, and telegraphed
a proposal to Number Two. She replied, "Yes. Am

coming at once with my mother." But by the next post came a letter from Number One saying, "I've changed my mind, and I'm coming." In a frenzy he telegraphed Number Two: "Don't you think we've been a bit hasty? Oughtn't you to think it over carefully?" She telegraphed back, "Have thought it over and am coming." When Number Two arrived, whom he hadn't seen for some time, he scarcely recognized her. A year later they were divorced.

520 *That kill-joy which discriminates*
Recover what appreciates

> The critical intelligence
> Undermines the State's defence,
> While the loyal heart refuses
> To reform the State's abuses;
> Yet all Being needs the blind,
> All Becoming the unkind.

525 *Establish a real neighborhood*

"Fish," writes Dr. Noble, "left together in groups get to know one another personally. . . . They form social hierarchies. One fish can strike a second fish without being struck in return, and the second has the right of passing the blow to a third individual. . . . These Pecking Orders owe their existence not to strength but to psychic factors such as the period of residence in an arca. Many fish devote most of their energies to trying to change their social status. When the fore-brains of ordinary sociable minnows are removed, the fish leave school, become hermits. . . .

Strangely enough, such fish may seem in other respects more effective organisms than fish with intact brains. They respond to food more quickly, exhibit greater vigor in flight reactions, exhibit less caution . . . but their social reactions are completely lost."

Quoted in *Time Magazine*. August 31, 1939.

527 *An ordre du cœur*

His father was a liberal politician and very anti-Nazi. His mother, who was divorced from his father, spent much of her time in Germany and was very anti-semitic. Yet, when he married a rich Jewess, his father was furious and his mother delighted.

540 *Flaubert didn't say*
    Of artists: Ils sont dans le vrai
He said it of peasants.

542 *Democracy? Ask Baudelaire*

La croyance au progrès est une doctrine de paresseux; une doctrine de Belges. C'est l'individu qui compte sur ses voisins pour faire sa besogne.

La vrai civilization n'est pas dans le gaz, ni dans la vapeur, ni dans les tables tournantes. Elle est dans la diminution des traces du péché original.

Baudelaire. *Mon Coeur Mis à Nu.*

545 *In crowds I am a friend of myth.*

From a letter quoted in Werner Jaeger, *Aristotle*

Le plaisir d'être dans les foules est une expression
mystérieuse de la jouissance de la multiplication du
nombre.

Baudelaire. Fusées

551 *O Seligkeit der Kreatur*

O Seligkeit der kleinen Kreatur
die immer bleibt im Schoosse, der sie austrug:
o Glück der Mücke, die noch immer hüpft,
selbst wenn sie Hochzeit hat: denn Schooss ist alles.

R. M. Rilke. Duino Elegies VIII

. . . womb

553 *In English, is a rhyme to tomb*

Do we want to return to the womb? Not at all.
No one really desires the impossible.
That is only the image out of our past
We practical people use when we cast
Our eyes on the future, to whom freedom is
The absence of all dualities.
Since there never can be much of that for us
In the universe of Copernicus,
Any heaven we think it decent to enter
Must be Ptolemaic with ourselves at the centre.

556 *Isolde's Sehnsucht for the dark*

e.g. Isolde. Barg im Busen
          Uns sich die Sonne,
          Leuchten lachend
          Sterne der Wonne.

Wagner. Tristan und Isolde. Act II Scene 2

559 *The great schismatic*

The serpent could not eat of the Tree of the Knowledge of Good and Evil himself: he could only tempt Eve to do so. He could still go naked.

560 *First split creation into two*

The Devil's philosophy in all its forms starts out from a dualistic division between, either the whole and its parts, or one part of the whole and the others. One part is good with absolute right to exist unchanged: the other is evil with no right to exist at all. Progress consists in a struggle between the two in which Good is victorious, and salvation is only attained with the complete annihilation of Evil, i.e. in a static monism.

As Blake pointed out, Dualism is the result of thinking about the creation in terms of a man's practical experience of human politics.

"King James was Bacon's Primum Mobile. . . . A tyrant is the worst disease and the cause of all others."

563 *Diversity in unity*

There are not "good" and "evil" existences. All existences are good, i.e., they have an equal right and an equal obligation to be and become.

No existence is without relation to and influence upon all other existences.

Evil is not an existence but a state of disharmony between existences. Pure evil would be pure passivity, a denial by an existence of any relation with any other existence; this is impossible because it would also mean a denial of its own existence.

Moral good is not an existence but an act, a rearrangement of existence which lessens or removes a disharmony.

589 *Polysyllabic oratory*

Base words are uttered only by the base
And can, as such, be clearly understood:
But noble platitudes—ah, there's a case
When the most careful scrutiny is needed
To tell the orator who's really good
From one who's base but merely has succeeded.

605 *Putting an end to them by action*

i.e., "Active evil is better than Passive good." (Blake)
It is not possible for an action to be evil in its original intention, for that would be to deny the right to exist of that part of the creation which is its agent; nor is it possible for an action to be evil in its ultimate effect for the effects of an act are infinite and that would mean that a single act could destroy all the previous regularities in the universe, and it would, in fact, be impossible to observe any such regularities. An act is evil in so far as it is misdirected and therefore fails to achieve its primal intention directly, but, instead, achieves it only by a roundabout series of mutually negating collisions ·and reactions. . . . Misdirection of intention is possible because the agent is unaware of or misinformed as to the true nature and extent of its relations with other agents, which amounts to saying that it is unaware of or misinformed as to its own nature.

607 *Man could do evil but not sin*

To do evil is to act contrary to self-interest. It is possible for all living creatures to do this because their knowledge of their self-interest is false or inadequate. Thus the animals whose evolution is complete, whose knowledge of their relations to the rest of creation is fixed, can do evil, but they cannot sin.

But we, being divided, remembering, evolving beings composed of a number of "selves," each with its false conception of its self-interest, sin in most that we do, for we can rarely act in such a way that the false self-interests of all our different "selves" are satisfied. The majority of our actions are in the false interest of one of those selves, not always the same one, at the expense of the rest. The consciousness that we are acting contrary to the interest of the others is our consciousness of sin. That is why, when we look at history and men, we always find evidence of guilt, but the objects and actions about which it is felt vary so widely that the only generalization we can make with certainty is of the universality of guilt, i.e., that conceptions of self-interest vary but are always false.

For, if our different "selves" had true self-knowledge of their respective self-interests, it would be impossible for us to act except in a way that satisfied them all, and we should each become not only an undivided consciousness and therefore, like the animals, unable to sin, but also an undivided consciousness with a true knowledge of itself, and therefore unable to do evil.

107

629 *The bottom of the graves*
A phrase of Blake's.
(Quoted by W. B. Yeats in *A Vision*.)

636 *Treat babe and bath-water the same*

Are not most neuroses the consequence of so drawing a false general conclusion from a true particular instance (the traumatic experience)?

*   *   *

Once for candy cook had stolen
X was punished by Papa;
When he asked where babies came from
He was lied to by Mama.

Now the city streets are waiting
To mislead him, and he must
Keep an eye on aged beggars
Lest they strike him in disgust.

641 *The Word's temporal interference*

Miracles are not supernatural interferences with natural laws, for truth cannot be divided against itself. When our knowledge reaches a point where we can see a cause-effect relation between events, accurately enough to predict the future, we call it a natural law. Miracles are events which occur contrary to our prediction, usually events which we would like to happen, for we do not commonly speak of an evil miracle. Our prediction was false because our knowledge was imperfect.

Everything that happens is a witness to the truth: the special value of miracles is that they reveal the imperfection of our knowledge and stimulate us to search further; they induce humility and curiosity. A miracle has not borne its full fruit until it is understood and can be repeated at will, that is, until it has ceased to be a miracle.   *   *   *

When he was four years old, Johnny developed an exhibitionist habit of coming downstairs naked after he had been put to bed and dancing round the dining room. His parents were anxious not to make him worse by making too much fuss and decided that the best cure was to take no notice. One evening they had guests to dinner. They explained that it was probable that Johnny would go through his act and asked their guests to ignore him. Sure enough, down he came, danced round the room, and went back to bed.

Two days later he went to stay with his grandmother. "Granny," he said, "do you know what happened the other day? There is a box in Mummy's room called Vanishing Cream. I've always wanted to know what it was, so two nights ago I smeared myself all over with it and went downstairs while Mummy was having a party. And it worked. Nobody saw me."

655 *The Rights of Man*

One stanch upholder of these was engaged in the American Slave Trade. He christened his three slave-ships Liberté, Egalité, and Fraternité.

702 *Our jolly picnic on the heath*
    Of the agreeable

The Champion smiles—What Personality!
The Challenger scowls—How horrid he must be!

But let the Belt change hands and they change places—
Still from the same old corners come the same grimaces.

720 *Him-who-steals*

Politicians have always had a low opinion of human
nature, though few have been so honest about it as
Pericles: "You should remember also that what you are
fighting against is not merely slavery as an exchange
for independence, but also a loss of empire and danger
from the animosities incurred in the exercise. . . .
For what you hold is, to speak somewhat plainly, a
tyranny; to take it, perhaps, was wrong, but to let it go
is unsafe. . . . Such qualities (quiet and lack of am-
bition) are useless to an imperial city."
Thucydides. *History of the Peloponnesian War.*

But if their experience were all; if all human be-
havior was like that of the Athenians toward the
Melians, the human race would long ago have become
extinct.

723 *By Man the Tough Devourer sets*
The nature his despair forgets

"One portion of being is the Prolific, the other the
Devouring. . . . The Prolific world ceases to be pro-
lific unless the Devourer, as a sea received the excess
of his delights . . .
"These two classes of men are always upon earth
and they should be enemies: whoever tries to recon-
cile them seeks to destroy existence."
William Blake. *The Marriage of Heaven and Hell.*

Man the Maker, i.e., man in his relation to the non-human world as cultivator, herdsman, engineer, discovered very early that it is useless to make moral judgments about Nature, to punish her or ever to try to coerce her, and that practical freedom means consciousness of practical necessity.

If it is hard for the Rich Man to enter into the Kingdom of Heaven, this is not because wealth or even its possession is an evil, but because the typical rich man can only be a consumer, not a producer and consumer, like the poor man. His knowledge of human nature is therefore limited to the knowledge of Man the Politician, i.e., man in his relations with other men, to that sphere of action where the nature of freedom is less understood. He is not totally without understanding, for he, like all men, had parents, but it is harder for him to accept it than for the poor who share his knowledge of Man the Politician, but know Man the Maker as well, and so have a double source of illumination, one from their childhood and one from their adult practical life.

* * *

These public men who seem so to enjoy their dominion,
With their ruined faces and their voices treble with hate,
Are no less martyred because unaware of their fetters:
What would *you* be like were you never allowed to create
Or reflect, but compelled to give an immediate opinion,
Condemned to destroy or distribute the works of your betters?

760 *No Codex Gentium we make*
Is difficult for Truth to break

"Where there is no strain, there is no history. . . . A metaphysician who comes to his subject from a general grounding in history will know that he must look for it. He will expect the various presuppositions he is studying to be consupponible only under pressure, the constellation being subject to certain strains and kept together by dint of a certain compromise or mutual toleration. . . . The ambition of 'deductive' metaphysics is to present a constellation of absolute presuppositions as a strainless structure like a body of propositions in mathematics.

"That is all right in mathematics because mathematical propositions are not historical propositions. But it is all wrong in metaphysics. A reformed metaphysics will conceive any given constellation of absolute presuppositions as having in its structure, not the simplicity and calm that characterizes the subject-matter of mathematics, but the intricacy and restlessness that characterize the subject-matter, say, of legal or constitutional history."

R. G. Collingwood. Metaphysics

762 *The Lex Abscondita*

Natural law is not to be confused with human political law. The latter is a generalized will imposed by force upon particular wills. If it is broken it does not cease to be the law. Human law rests upon Force and Belief, i.e., belief in this rightness.

In Natural law, on the other hand, there can be no

opposition between the will of the whole and the separate wills of the parts. It is simply what happens in the field under consideration if there is no interference from outside. Our knowledge of Natural Law is derived from an observation of particulars. If we find a single exception, it means that our formulation of Natural Law has been incorrect.

There is therefore no Natural Philosophy, only a Natural Way. The way rests upon Faith and Doubt: Faith that Natural Law exists and that we can have knowledge of it; Doubt that our knowledge can ever be perfect or unmixed with error.

Our grounds for Faith: the unhappiness of **Man**

Our grounds for doubt: the same

(Definition. I believe $X = I$ believe the proposition X to be true.

I have faith in $X =$ The existence of X is, for me, an absolute presupposition.

I doubt $X = I$ admit the possibility that, at some future unspecified date, and for reasons also unspecified, I may come

either to believe the proposition X to be false

or to find that, for me, the presupposition that X exists is no longer absolute but relative.)

*   *   *

The Hidden Law does not deny
Our laws of probability,
But takes the atom and the star
And human beings as they are,
And answers nothing when we lie.

113

It is the only reason why
No government can codify,
And legal definitions mar
      The Hidden Law.

Its utter patience will not try
To stop us if we want to die;
When we escape It in a car,
When we forget It in a bar,
These are the ways we're punished by
      The Hidden Law.

778 *Afraid to be themselves or ask*
    What acts are proper to their task

Two students went to a left-wing demonstration with
a home-made banner bearing the initials W.K.N.W.
A.B.Q. When asked what these stood for, they replied:
    We Know Nothing Whatever About Basic Questions,
The banner was hastily confiscated and they were
given another one saying: Culture for the Masses.

         *   *   *

Extract from a college play about the Spanish Civil War
    (Scene. Two loyalist militiamen in a shell-hole dur-
ing a battle)—"It's all right, Juan; the American stu-
dents will help us."

799. *How's our Socialist this morning*

Fascism is Socialism that has lost faith in the future.
It's slogan is Now or Never. In demanding a dictator
it is really demanding the advent of the Good Life on
earth through a supernatural miracle.

804 *Such things have happened in the lives*
    Of all the best conservatives

Which was the real politician, the active Buonoparte
Who altered the map of Europe and broke his heart
Or his heartless police dog, the passive Fouché
Why betrayed what he called "Un acteur usé"?

818 *The vorpal sword of an Agrarian*

Hans-in-Kelder, Hans-in-Kelder,
    What are you waiting for?
We need your strong arm to look after the farm
    And keep the wolf from the door.

Hans-in-Kelder, Hans-in-Kelder,
    Came out of the parsley-bed,
Came out at a run and leveled a gun
    And shot his old parents dead.

821 *The either-ors, the mongrel halves*
    i.e., the impatient romantics.
    (Definition of Romanticism. Unawareness of the
        dialectic.)

The cause of romanticism is either laziness or im-
patience. The lazy romantic is too woolly-minded to
recognize a paradox when he meets one, like the stu-
dent who, when asked in an ethics class to give his views
on punishment, replied he was in favor of light Capital
Punishment. The impatient romantic sees more
clearly, but sees only one side of the paradox; the
other he ignores or denies. Professor A. E. Housman's
comment upon a certain textual editor is the classic

description of this type. "He is like a donkey between two bundles of hay who fondly imagines that if one bundle of hay be removed, he will cease to be a donkey."

829 *There lies the gift of double focus*

The Devil, indeed, is the father of Poetry, for poetry might be defined as the clear expression of mixed feelings. The poetic mood is never indicative.

*   *   *

Whether determined by God or their neural structure, still
All men have one common creed, account for it as you will:
The Truth is one and incapable of self-contradiction;
All knowledge that conflicts with itself is Poetic Fiction.

PART III

851 *The erotic and the logical*

In *Le Bourgeois,* Soubart divides men into the erotics and the bourgeois.

(Quoted by Maritain in
Freedom in the Modern World)

856 *Our privileged community*

"Don't let's pity ourselves. We are the privileged. Our minds are lit by gas. There are so many people who are shivering in attics without even candles."

Flaubert. (Quoted by Francis
Steegmüller in *Flaubert and Madame Bovary*)

864 *The temenos' small wicket stands*

". . . the region of taboo, the temenos, which in ancient times signified a piece of land or a grove consecrated to the god . . . The image of the temenos with the well-spring developed in Islamic architecture, under early Christian influence, into the court of the mosque and the ritualistic washing place located in the centre. We have the same thing in the Occidental cloister with the well in the garden."

Carl Jung. *The Integration of Personality.*

878 *With the Eternal Innocence*

"Eternity is the complete and perfect possession of unlimited life all at once."
                              Boethius.

*   *   *

"Eternity, that is, the infinite enjoyment of existence."
                    Spinoza. *Correspondence.*

898 *Hell is the being of the lie*

It is possible that the gates of Hell are always standing wide open. The lost are perfectly free to leave whenever they like, but to do so would mean admitting that the gates were open, that is, that there was another life outside. This they cannot admit, not because they have any pleasure in their present existence, but because the life outside would be different and, if they admitted its existence, they would have to lead it. They know this. They know that they are free to leave and they know why they do not. This knowledge is the flame of hell.

914 *Heaven where*
    Is perfect freedom.

"Grigorovich has never been a caretaker in the docks; that is why he holds the Kingdom of Heaven so cheaply. He is fibbing."
            Anton Tchekov. *Letter to A. S. Souvorin*

*   *   *

"The Kingdom of Heaven is within"—then, as
In there the wills of the Many have always been done,

May the same come true out here for the will of the
   One.
That each may only desire what he already has."

922 *Whom we adore but do not trust*

"Love to life is still possible—only one loves differently.
It is the love to a woman that causes us doubts."
                    Nietzsche. *Nietzsche contra Wagner.*

926 *Time is sin and can forgive*

Forgiveness of sin does not mean that the effect of an
act is annulled, but that we are shown what that effect
is. This knowledge, that we have been punished but
not judged, removes our burden of guilt, for guilt is,
in part, ignorance of the exact effect of our act upon
others and, in part, a dread that upon ourselves it has
had no effect at all, that we are so unimportant as to
be beneath the notice of the Divine justice, that, as
we have not been punished, we must do what God
never does, judge the past.

   To judge is to take a decision, and we made the
wrong judgment once and for all in the instant of com-
mitting the act. Once committed, the act is an irrevo-
cable part of our past, and can no longer be regarded
ethically, but only aesthetically, that is understood and
endured.

930 *Where any skyline we attain*
    Shows yet a higher ridge again

         The bear went over the mountain
         The bear went over the mountain

The bear went over the mountain
And what do you think he saw?

He saw another mountain
He saw another mountain
He saw another mountain
And what do you think he did?

The bear went over the mountain
Etc.
American Folk Song

962 *Our faith well balanced by our doubt*

"Nier, croire, et douter bein, son à l'homme ce que le
courir est au cheval."
Pascal. *Pensées*

* * *

With what conviction the young man spoke
When he thought his nonsense rather a joke:
Now, when he doesn't doubt any more,
No one believes the booming old bore.

970 *A reverent frivolity*

Froh—Lightly, without cursing love, were it (the
treasure) won.

Loge—Just so. Without guile, as in children's games.
Wagner. *Das Rheingold.*

974 *Its sad nostalgie des adieux*

Because I know that time is always time
And place is always and only place
And what is actual is actual only for one time
And only for one place

I rejoice that things are as they are and
I renounce the blessed face
And renounce the voice.

           T. S. Eliot. *Ash Wednesday*

990 *To particles who claim the field*

Standing among the ruins the horror-struck conqueror
exclaimed:
"Why do they have to attempt to refuse me my destiny?
Why?"

991 *Nor trust the demagogue who raves*

When statesmen gravely say—"We must be realistic—"
The chances are they're weak and therefore pacifistic:
But when they speak of Principles—look out—perhaps
Their generals are already poring over maps.

996 *Need not be, orators, for you*

    Failure is isolationist
    And loyal to itself alone;
    The Promising and the Half-grown
    Who feel their young ambitions thwarted
    Beneath some national flag enlist;
    Success has never not been known
    To intervene and be exported.

1059 *Two worlds, describing their rewards*
      That one in tangents, this in chords

Ordnung und Frieden und Glück hat das Land
Wo die Recht' hat Vernunft und die Link' hat
      Verstand.   (after Möller von der Bruck.)

"Heartless Cynics," the young men shout,
Blind to the world of Fact without:
"Silly Dreamers," the old men grin,
Deaf to the world of Purpose within.

*　　*　　*

New Facts will not be known
Until we part and live once more alone:
New Values not be found
Until we meet again on common ground.

1062 *Here all are kings, there each a brother*

He whose youth was full of shrouds
Will deteriorate in crowds;
He whose childish lot was thrown
With angels will decay alone

*　　*　　*

It is the extrovert who is often without a social con-
science. The introvert can never lose his; he can only
pervert it into contempt, crime or ambition to become
a dictator. Politically this is the age of the great, mad
introverts.

1063 *In politics the Fall of Men*

The Garden of Eden: the Golden Age. This does
not mean that there was once a time when Man did
not do evil, but only that there was once a time when
he did not sin, i.e., when society was relatively so
closed that freedom was confined to obedience to
causal necessity, i.e., to the aesthetic endurance of
tribulation, and there was little or no need of ethical

122

resistance to temptation, when human law was not felt as coercive but regarded as a perfect codification of Natural Law, when, in fact, it was still possible to live by beliefs and not yet necessary to live by Faith.

1066 *Like Burke, to think them both the same*

"La tyrannie est de vouloir avoir par une voie ce qu' on ne peut avoir que par une autre.

Pascal. *Pensées*

1138 *The Terrible, the Merciful, the Mothers*

Mephistopheles—
    Ungern entdeck ich höheres Geheimnis.—
    Göttinnen thronen hehr in Einsamkeit,
    Um sie kein Ort, noch weniger eine Zeit;
    Von ihnen sprechen ist Verlegenheit.
    Die Mütter sind es!
            Goethe. *Faust.* Part II. Act I. Scene 5.

1141 *The deep Urmutterfurcht that drives*

Wotan—Hinab, denn, Erda
        Urmutter Furcht
        Ursorge
        Zum ewigen Schlaf
        Hinab, hinab.
            Wagner. *Siegfried.* Act III. Scene 1.

1145 *Das Weibliche that bids us come*

Chorus Mysticus—Das Ewig-Weibliche
            Zieht uns hinan.
        Goethe. *Faust.* Part II. Act V. Scene 7.

1149 *O deine Mutter kehrt dir nicht*

Brunnhilde—Du wonniges Kind
            deine Mutter kehrt dir nicht wieder
            Du selbst bin ich der mich selige liebst....

Siegfried—Brach sie mein Bild
            so brenn ich nur selbst.
                Wagner. *Siegfried.* Act III. Scene 2.

1164 *We are conscripts to our age*

—"Don't you dream of a world, a society with no coercion?"
—"Yes, where a foetus is able to refuse to be born."

1167 *With Polycarp's despairing cry*

"In what century hast thou caused me to be born, O my God."

1168 *Desert or become ill*

"Sickness is always the answer when we are inclined to doubt concerning our right to *our* task, when we begin to make it easier for ourselves in any respect."
                Nietzsche. *The Case of Wagner.*

*   *   *

"Sometime or other in the course of the treatment I am accustomed to call my patient's attention to the fact that from the human semen and ovum there is born, not a dog, nor a cat, but a human being, that there is some force within the germ which is able to fashion a nose, a finger, a brain, that accordingly this force, which carries out such marvelous processes, might well produce a headache, or diahorrea or an inflamed throat, that indeed I do not suppose it unreasonable to suppose that it can even manufacture pneumonia or gout or cancer. I dare to go so far with my patients as to maintain that the force really does such things, that according to its pleasure it makes people ill for specific ends, that according to its pleasure it selects for such ends the place, the time and the nature of the illness. Thus it implants on the loving mouth which is yearning for kisses, a disfiguring eczema; if in spite of that I am kissed, then indeed I shall be happy, but if the kiss is not forthcoming, then it is not because I am unloved, but because of the revolting eczema. . . . And then I ask the patient, Why have you a nose? To smell with, he replies. So I say, your It has given you a cold in order that you shall not smell something or other. Find out what it is you are not to smell. And now and again the patient will actually find out some smell which he wants to escape, and you need not believe it, but I do—when he has found it, the cold disappears. . . ."

Georg Groddeck. *The Book of the It.*

1213 *Luther's faith*

With conscience cocked to listen for the thunder
He saw the Devil busy in the wind,
Over the chiming steeples and then under
The doors of nuns and doctors who had sinned.

What apparatus could stave off disaster
Or cut the brambles of man's error down?

Flesh was a silent dog that bites its master,
World a still pond in which its children drown.

The fuse of Judgment spluttered in his head:
"Lord, smoke these honeyed insects from their hives;
All Works, Great Men, Societies, are bad;
The Just shall live by Faith . . ." he cried in dread.

And men and women of the world were glad
Who never trembled in their useful lives.

1213 *Montaigne's doubt*

Outside his library window he could see
A gentle landscape terrified of grammar,
Cities where lisping was compulsory
And provinces where it was death to stammer.

The hefty lay exhausted. O it took
This donnish undersexed conservative
To start a revolution, and to give
The Flesh its weapons to defeat the Book.

When devils drive the reasonable wild,
They strip their adult century so bare,
Love must be regrown from the sensual child:

To doubt becomes a way of definition,
Even belles lettres legitimate as prayer,
And laziness an act of pure contrition.

1220 *Emerged a new Anthropos*

"Luther set up the highest spiritual principle: pure
inwardness. It may become so dangerous that in Prot-
estantism a point may be reached at which worldliness

126

is honoured and highly valued as piety. And this—as I maintain—cannot happen in Catholicism.

"But why can it not happen in Catholicism? Because Catholicsm has the universal premise that we men are pretty well rascals. And why can it happen in Protestantism? Because the Protestant principle is related to a particular premise: a man who sits in the anguish of death, in fear and trembling and much tribulation—and of those there are not many in any one generation."

Journals of Soren Kierkegaard.

1221 *Empiric Economic Man*

"Middletown believes:

—That progress is a law of life.

—That men won't work if they don't have to. 'Work is not fun. None of us would do a lick of work if he didn't have to.'

—That too much education and contact with books and big ideas unfit a person for practical life.

—That schoolteachers are usually people who couldn't make good in business.

—That leisure is a fine thing, but work comes first.

—That all of us hope we'll get to the place some time where we can work less and have more time to play.

—But that it is wrong for a man to retire when he is still able to work. 'What will he do with all his time?'

—That 'culture and things like that' are more the business of women than of men.

—That leisure is something you spend with people and a person is 'queer' who enjoys solitary leisure.

—That a person doesn't want to spend his leisure

doing 'heavy' things or things that remind him of the 'unpleasant side of life.'

—But that leisure should be spent in wholesomely 'worth-while' things and not just be idle or frivolous.

—That it is better to be appreciative than discriminating.

—That anything widely acclaimed is pretty apt to be good.

—That Christianity is the final form of religion and all other religions are inferior to it.

—But that which you believe is not so important as the kind of person you are.

—That preachers are rather impractical people who wouldn't be likely to make really good in business.

—That I wouldn't want my son to go into the ministry.

—That preachers should stick to religion and not try to talk about business, public affairs, and other things 'they don't know anything about.' "

R. S. and H. M. Lynd. *Middletown in Transition.*

1223 *Profit his rational incentive*

A New York psychologist tells me that when the Stock Market crashed in 1929, many business men suddenly became sexually impotent.

1224 *And work his whole exercitus*

During the course of a successful career, he had held many jobs. When asked how he had liked one of them, he replied, "I never like or dislike any job. Work is the element in which I breathe."

How to live without working is the goal
Of every child who loves its mother
For in "work" the energies of the soul
Are sapped by the will of another.

1232 *Proved some assumptions were untrue*

Though all our ideas, true or false, are the product of our experience, that is, of our way of living, it is legitimate to see in our ideas the prime agents of human historical change, for, were it not for his capacity to think, man's evolution would be complete like that of the animals.

Any idea has two practical purposes, to justify our satisfactions, and to suggest a way to relieve our wants. As justification, an idea is a pure reflection of our material life and cannot re-enter history as an effective agent because it does not want to. As a means to relieve wants, it demands a change in our behavior and so becomes an agent of historical change. In so far as it is true, that is, achieves its conscious intention, the cause-effect relation between idea and historical change is obvious, for example, in the historical effects of technical inventions. In so far as it is false, though it is just as active an agent as if it were true, the effects which it produces are so different from its conscious intention that we fail to detect the cause-effect relation and see only its justificatory purpose, the more so because, since the principal obstacle to true thinking is our desire for justification, the falser an idea the more obvious its justificatory element.

As far as I know, Kierkegaard was the first to distinguish accurately between *tribulations,* all the troubles that come upon us from without and can't be disposed of by acts of will but can only be endured, that is, treated aesthetically; and *temptations,* all the internal conflicts that must not be endured but solved in action by the will, that is, treated ethically. Further, he was the first to include among tribulations, not only physical disasters like flood, fire and famine, but also all images, impulses, feelings of guilt that rise from the subconscious.

Considered as practical applied activities, all sciences have as their aim the transformation of tribulations into temptations. Why is this desirable? Because it turns an insoluble problem of passive endurance into a soluble problem of conduct, an aesthetic into an ethical problem.

The true purpose of psychotherapy

Imagine a young man tormented by fantasies of cutting women's throats. He is horrified and tries to suppress them. This method fails. They get worse. He suffers till, in his despair, he goes to a psychologist and with his help unravels his complex and is 'cured' i.e., the fantasies cease and his desire for women becomes "normal." Presently he falls in love with a married woman. Now he suffers again, torn between desire and conscience, but this time no psychologist can help him. He has to choose—Shall I or shall I not break up this home?—and the decision lies with his will and his will alone. In a sense his suffering is worse than before, since it is less painful to endure what you do not like but know you cannot prevent than to do what you do not like when you know you could do otherwise.

Why is psychology dangerous?

Because it tempts a man to think that since the suffering of his tribulation can be removed, he will not have to suffer at all; that, since the way to cure tribulations is to treat them aesthetically, that is, not to repress them by will but to admit them and examine them, temptations can be dealt with in the same way by yielding to them.

But the ethical justification of psychotherapy as of all applied sciences is simply this: It is always sinful presumption for man to endure more than he has to, or to imagine that he is more extraordinary than he really is. Nevertheless, he will always have much to endure and he will always be extraordinary.

Judge not

No one can separate in another's suffering how much is tribulation and how much is temptation. Therefore others must be regarded aesthetically and only oneself ethically. (Except ye become as little children. . . .)

1245 *Reason's depravity*

"The absolute position of the knowing subject became doubtful when the break which the Middle Ages sought between nature and super-nature was found in nature itself, and when super-nature was done away with, as happened in Protestantism. While the Protestant interpretation of life, like the whole Renaissance, has a new affirmative attitude towards nature, in contrast to the Renaissance, it realises the deep contradictions in nature. It does not flee from it into supernature, as so the Middle Ages. It remains in nature, but it cannot remain naively in it, like Renaissance thought and Humanism, but remains in nature as the sphere of decision. The fundamental Protestant attitude is to stand in nature, taking upon oneself the inevitable reality; not to flee from it, either into the world of ideal forms or into the related world of super-nature, but to make decisions in concrete reality. Here the subject has no possibility of an absolute position. It cannot go out of the sphere of decision. Every part of its nature is affected by these contradictions. Fate and freedom reach into the act of knowledge and make it an historical deed: the Kairos determines the Logos."

Paul Tillich. *The Interpretation of History.*

*　　*　　*

In gorgeous robes befitting the occasion
For weeks their spiritual and temporal lordships met
To reconcile eternity with time and set
The earth of marriage on a sure foundation:
The little town was full of spies; corrupt mankind
Waited on tenterhooks of expectation.

The doors swung back at last: success had been complete.
The formulae essential to salvation
Were found for ever, and the true relation
Of Agape to Eros finally defined:

The burghers hung out flags in celebration,
The peasants danced and roasted oxen in the street.

As they dispersed, four heralds galloped up with news:

"The tribes are moving on the Western Marches.
Out East a virgin has conceived a son again.
The Southern harbours are infested with the Jews.
The Northern provinces are much deluded
By one who claims there are not seven stars, but ten."

Who wrote upon the council-chamber arches
That sad exasperated cry of tired old men:
—*Postremum Sanctus Spiritus effduit?*

1267 *went mad protesting*

"Cowper came to me and said: O that I were insane always. I will never rest. Can you not make me truly insane? I will never rest till I am so. You retain health, yet are as mad as any of us—mad as a refuge from unbelief, from Bacon, Newton and Locke."

William Blake.

1271 *Crucified by fools*

" 'Gustave Flaubert? Nothing but an eccentric,' a respectable Rouen business man once replied when asked his opinion. 'One day he's living quietly at Croisset, and the next day he packs his trunk and is off to Carthage. We don't like that sort of thing much, in Rouen.' "

Francis Steegmüller. *Flaubert and Madame Bovary.*

1274 *And play for safety all their lives*

Description of a prominent literary critic:
"He wanted to write poetry and ended up with seven jobs."

1275 *For whose Verbürgerlichung of*
     All joy and suffering and love

"Their ethics are a short summary of police ordinances . . . they have no conception of the point of view (which a gnostic set made its own) of getting to know the world through sin—and yet, they too say: one must sow one's wild oats; they have never even had a glimpse of the idea which is behind that saying, after one has forced one's way through the hidden and mysterious door into that 'dark realm of sighs' which in all its horror is only open to foreboding—when one sees the broken victims of seduction and inveiglement, and the tempter's coldness.
                    Journals of Soren Kierkegaard.

1277 *Let the grand pariah atone*

              La vraie grandeur des parias
                 Baudelaire. *Mon Coeur mis a nu.*

              *   *   *

Quand j'aurais inspiré le dégout et l'horreur universels, j'aurais conquis la solitude.
                          Baudelaire. *Fusées.*

              *   *   *

The great error of the Romantics was their failure to recognize that the bourgeois were not real devils but false angels. The answer to those who do noble

actions from base motives is not, as some of them
seem to have imagined, to try to do base actions from
noble motives, nor is a parody of order unmasked by
a deliberate chaos.

*　　　*　　　*

Only God can tell the saintly from the suburban,
Counterfeit virtues always resemble the true;
Neither in Life nor Art is honesty bohemian,
The free behave much as the respectable do.

*　　　*　　　*

The intellectuals have, unfortunately, done their
full share in bringing about a popular anti-intellectual
revolt under the banner of morality.

*　　　*　　　*

To the man-in-the-street, who, I'm sorry to say,
　　Is a keen observer of life,
The word Intellectual suggests straight away
　　A man who's untrue to his wife.

1281 *Their grapevine rumor would grow true*

"Ai-je besoin de dire que le peu qui restera de politique
se débattra peniblement dans les étreintes de l'ani-
malité génerale, et que les gouverants seront forcées,
pour se maintenir et pour créer un fantôme d'ordre,
recourir à des moyens qui feraient frissoner notre
humanité actuelle, pourtant si endurcie?"

Baudelaire. *Fusées.*

1288 *The measurable taking charge
Of him who measures*

A Ph.D. student approached a professor of philosophy

with these words. "I am making a comparative study of the academic standards in American universities. I am doing this by comparing the number of pages of required reading in each major subject. Could you tell me what the number is in philosophy at your college?"

"But, surely," said the professor, "fifty pages of Aristotle in Greek is not the same as fifty pages of a popular history of philosophy."

"That," the student replied, "is a matter of opinion. The number of pages is a matter of fact."

*   *   *

A brilliant young man was commissioned by a magazine to write the definitive three thousand words on Henry Ford. After spending weeks at Detroit, he returned and shut himself up in a small office with a glass door through which the curious could watch the papers piling up around his feet. Weeks went by. The dead-line came; he asked for an extension, then another, then another. Finally the editor lost patience and demanded the article by noon next day.

As the clock began striking the young man came out carrying a single sheet of paper. There was an awed hush in the office as the editor took it. It bore only one sentence:

Ford is a foetus in the womb of General Motors.

The young man retired to a sanatorium.

301 *And idiots by enormous sums*

"Enormous sums are death and therefore not from God." Vaslav Nijinsky, *Diary.*

1306 *Die Aufgeregten*

The title of a play by Goethe.

The German refugee, who was still in this thirties, had had an exciting youth—in the Black Reichswehr, in the Nazi movement. As a supporter of Otto Strasser he quarreled with the Nazis and fought with the Loyalists in Spain. When asked if he had ever been happy, he said: "Yes. There was a peasant rising in Bavaria. We threw bombs."

1316 *What Persian apparatus*

> Persicos, odi, puer, apparatus.
> Horace. *Odes*. Book I. Ode 38.

1346 *Find faults at which to hang the head*

"Young people err so often and so grievously: that they (in whose nature it lies to have no patience) cast themselves upon each other, when love takes possession of them, scatter themselves just as they are, in all their untidiness, disorder, confusion . . . And then what? What has life to do with this heap of half-battered existence which they call their common living and which they would gladly call their happiness, if it were possible, and their future? Thus each loses himself for the sake of the other and loses the other and many others that were yet to come."
> R. M. Rilke. *Letters to a Young Poet*.

1363 *If all his agents are untrue*

According to researches at Chicago and Cornell, a chemical engineer has a five to one chance of a happy marriage, a traveling salesman, only a fifty-fifty chance.

1367 *The average of the average man*
Becomes the dread Leviathan.

> Who built the Prison State?
> Free-men hiding from their fate.
> Will wars ever cease?
> Not while they leave themselves in peace.

1371 *The gross behavior of a group*

"Hard cases make bad law," as the politician learns to his cost:

Yet just is the artist's reproach— "Who generalizes is lost."

1378 *In Plato's lie of intellect*

"When it is necessary to make a tyrant out of *reason,* as Socrates did, there must be a considerable danger of something else playing the tyrant. . . . The fanaticism with which the whole of Greek Thought throws itself upon rationality betrays a desperate situation: They were in danger, they had only one choice: they had either to go to ruin or be *absurdly rational.* The moralism of Greek philosophers from Plato downwards is pathologically conditioned; their estimation of dialectics likewise. Reason-virtue-happiness means only that we have to imitate Socrates and put a permanent *daylight* in opposition to the obscure desires— the daylight of reason. We have to be rational, clear and distinct, at any price: every yielding to the instincts, to the unconscious, leads *downwards.*"

Nietzsche. *The Problem of Socrates.*

1379 *That all are weak but the Elect*

> What will cure the nation's ill?
> A leader with a selfless will.
> But how can you find this leader of yours?
> By a process of Natural Selection of course.

1381. *For, knowing Good, they will no Wrong*

> To know the Good, you say, is to will it?
> But with some the immediate reaction is: Kill it.

1384 *Rousseau's falsehood of the flesh*

> "Rousseau thought men good by nature: he found
> them evil and made no friend."
>
> > William Blake.

      *   *   *

"The reading of your book makes us want to creep on all fours. However, since it is now more than sixty years since I lost that habit, I feel unfortunately that it is impossible for me to take it up again, and I leave that natural aptitude to those who are more worthy of it than you or I. Neither can I embark to go and live with the savages of Canada. The ailments with which I am afflicted retain me by the side of the greatest doctor of Europe, and I could not find the same attentions among the Missouri Indians."

> Voltaire. *Letter to Rousseau.*

      *   *   *

"*My impracticables*—Rousseau, or return to nature *in impuris naturalibus. Schiller,* or the moral trumpeter of Säckingen—*Kant* or *cant* as an intelligible character

—Victor Hugo, or Pharos in a sea of absurdity*—Liszt,*
or the school of running—after women*—George Sand,*
or *lactea ubertas; i.e., the milk-cow with 'the fine style'*
—Michelet, or enthusiasm which strips off the coat—
Carlyle, or pessimism as an undigested dinner*—Les
frères de Goncourt,* or the two Ajaxes struggling with
Homer. Music by Offenbach*—Zola,* or 'the delight to
stink.' "

Nietzsche. *Roving Expeditions
of an Inopportune Philosopher.*

1387 *And strong in the Irrational*

—What should the citizen's motto be?
—One for All and All for One.
—And the national policy?
—To fight for a dominant place in the sun.

1388 *The social lie*

"Every voter is the conscious
Master of his soul:
Overthrow the tyrant whole;
Free are the Dissociated."

"Passive soldiers make a people
Master of its fate:
Selfish parts are never great;
Free, though, is the Integrated."

The selfish and the tyrants die:
Great are those who master by
Conscious passivity;
Free the differentiated.

1402 *Not as a gift from life with which*
To serve, enlighten and enrich.

"Nor Creator nor creature, my son, was ever without
love, either natural or rational; and this thou knowest.
The natural is always without error; but the other may
err through an evil object, or through too little or
too much vigour. . . .

Hence thou mayst understand that love must be the
seed of every virtue in you, and of every deed that
deserves punishment."

Dante. *Purgatorio*. Canto XVII.

1432 *The genius of the loud Steam Age*

"The Wagnerian heroines, each and all, when one
has only stripped them of their heroic trappings, are
like counterparts of Madame Bovary. . . . Yes, taken
as a whole, Wagner appears to have no interest in any
other problems than those which at present interest
pretty Parisian *décadents,* always just five steps from
the hospital. Nothing but quite modern problems,
nothing but problems of a *great* city."

Nietzsche. *The Case of Wagner.*

* * *

Wagner is the greatest of the Romantic artists, be-
cause he carries the Romantic heresy—the exaltation
of causal necessity over logical necessity—further than
any other. The only character in *The Ring* who shows
any sign of logic is Fricka and she is made unsym-
pathetic. As studies in tribulation, as psycho-analytic
case histories, the operas are masterpieces. As dramatic

141

plots they are absurd, and absurd not because the characters make mistakes for which later they have to suffer, but because they know *beforehand* that they are mistakes. In *Oedipus Rex* the tragic effect lies in the contrast between the knowledge of the *audience* and the ignorance of the *actors*. In *The Ring*, on the other hand, the actors are never tired of explaining to the audience exactly what is going to happen and how awful it will be; i.e., their actions deny their knowledge and, even as psychology, that is absurd.

For instance, Walhalla is burnt because it is surrounded by faggots made from the World-Ash-tree. Why does Wotan have such dangerously inflammable material there? If Wotan knows that his power depends on keeping treaties, why does he build Walhalla in the first place? If Wotan is able to create a saving race who hate the gods, why does he have to give way to Fricka? If Wotan knows that all he fashions are slaves, why does he choose to beget them, or if he so chooses, why does he mind? Wotan says: "Though the gods are ending, I feel no anguish, since it works my will." If this is the case, why does he draw it out so? Why does Alberich forswear love when he already does not love? (He still remains capable of lust, for he begets Hagen.)

These are only a few questions out of many, and the answer to all of them is the same. *To allow Wagner to go on writing music and, moreover, the kind of music that he was good at writing.* The real motto of all his characters is: *The show must go on.* Nowhere else in the history of art (his greatest rival is Proust) is the contrast so striking between the helplessness of the characters and the amazing will-power, the capacity for self-help, the mendicant charm, of their creator. Why? Because of the peculiar nature of Wagner's talent. In the expression of suffering, physical suffering (Amfortas), the suffering of unrequited love (Hans Sachs), the suffering of self-love (Tristan. For it is clear that his wound prevents him from going to bed with Isolde), the suffering of betrayed love (Brunnhilde), the sufferings, in short, of failure, Wagner is perhaps the greatest genius who ever lived. But in the expression of suffering only. Happiness, social life, mystical joy, *success* were completely beyond him. His finest passages are monologues, his "happy" duet, the finale of *Siegfried* is his worst, and his crowd passages are disgustingly vulgar. Even the finale of *Die Meistersinger* suggests a military parade, something *unspontaneous*.

For spontaneous happiness, friendship, requited love, we must go elsewhere—to Mozart. No, if Wagner were to compose at all, i.e., if *he* were to be happy, his characters had to be unhappy.

For the strong, the intelligent, the healthy, the successful, those on whom, just because they are so, falls the duty of understanding weakness, stupidity, disease and failure in order that they may cure them, Wagner's operas are essential, a constant source of delight. They *must* listen to him.

But who should never be allowed to listen to Wagner? The unhappy, the disappointed, the politically ambitious, the self-pitying, those who imagine themselves misunderstood, the Wagnerians. And to whom should they be compelled to listen? To Mozart and Beethoven.

1449 *Their bothered day*

> It is the world's one crime its babes grow dull,
> Its poor are ox-like, limp and leaden-eyed.
> Not that they starve, but starve so dreamlessly,
> Not that they sow, but that they seldom reap,
> Not that they serve, but have no gods to serve,
> Not that they die, but that they die like sheep.
>
> Vachel Lindsay.

1458 *The secular cathedrals stand*

> What was that? Why are the public buildings so high? O,
> That is because the spirits of the public are so low.

*   *   *

> "The evolved tenement house had an evolved fire-proof staircase, scientific, impermeable to the microbe, and plated with goodly marble. This was a new style of poverty. Here the poor were fattened into food for the ogres."
>
> Henry James. *The American Scene*

1462 *Man is weak and has to die*

Main killing diseases in U.S.A. for 1937 (in %)

Whole population

Heart	23.9 (on the increase)
Influenza and Pneumonia	10.2
Cancer	9.0 (on the increase)

Infancy (0–4)

Injuries prior to birth	50.0
Influenza	26.9
Diarrhea and Enteritis	7.9

Youth (5–19)

Influenza	12.6
Accidents	10.9
Tuberculosis	9.6
Heart	6.4

Middle Age (20–59)

Heart	18.7
Cancer	
Influenza	

Suicides and maternity deaths important in this group

Old Age (60 and over)

Heart	33.9
Cancer	
Cerebral Hemorrhage	
Nephritis	

*　　　*　　　*

I sought my death and found it in my womb;
　　I looked for life, and saw it was a shade;
I trod the earth, and knew it was my tomb;
　　And now I die, and now I was but made:
My glass is full, and now my glass is run;
　　And now I live, and now my life is done.

Chidiock Tichborne.

145

1466 *Virgin before the Dynamo*

"As he grew accustomed to the great gallery of machines, he began to feel the forty-foot dynamos as a moral force, much as the early Christians felt the Cross. . . . Here opened another totally new education, which promised to be by far the most hazardous of all. The knife edge along which he must crawl, like Sir Launcelot in the twelfth century, divided two kingdoms of force which had nothing in common but attraction. They were as different as a magnet is from gravitation, supposing one knew what a magnet was, or gravitation, or love. The force of the Virgin was still felt at Lourdes, and seemed as potent as X-rays; but in America neither Venus nor Virgin ever had value as force—at most as sentiment. No American had ever been truly afraid of either."

The Education of Henry Adams.

1468 *Hat keine verfallenen Schlösser*

DEN VEREINIGTEN STAATEN

Amerika, du hast es besser
als unser Kontinent, das alte,
hast keine verfallenen Schlösser
und keine Basalte.
Dich stört nicht im Innern,
zu lebendiger Zeit,
unnützes Erinnern
und vergeblicher Streit.
Benutzt die Gegenwart mit Glück!
Und wenn nun eure Kinder dichten,

bewahre sie ein gut Geschick
Vor Ritter—Räuber—und Gespenstergeschichten.
                              Goethe. *Zahme Xenien.* IX.

1469 *The great Rome*
  Of all who lost or hated home

W, who comes of pioneer stock, tells me that, in the
case of his family, at least, the pioneer wanderlust was
a search for something that did not and could not exist
in America, and that men were farmers by circum-
stance, not by choice. Thus his great-grandfather was
the first settler to reach Wisconsin at the beginning of
the nineteenth century. He could, therefore, have the
pick of whatever piece of land he wished. The piece
he chose was very poor farming land, but an excellent
site for a gentleman's country house.

1483 *Pelagian versus Jansenist*

The evolution of all societies that have not stagnated
or perished has always been in the same direction, from
the closed towards the open, but this evolution has, so
far, always been accompanied by the development of
social and economic inequality, or, in other words, dif-
ferent classes have moved towards the open society
at different speeds. For the ruling class a society may
be relatively open while at the same time for the
working class it is relatively closed. The former will
always tend to rationalize, to ignore the existence of
causal necessity. They will blame the poor for suc-
cumbing (as they themselves do) to temptations, when

147

they are really succumbing to tribulations (imposed by the ruling class). They moralise. The poor, on the other hand, who have never been given the opportunity for logical choice, will always tend to deny its existence. Since their own behavior is due, in large measure, to the tribulation of being poor (Marxism) they will ascribe the behavior of the ruling class to the tribulations of being rich, when it is, in large measure, due to their moral failure to resist the temptations of wealth.

Thus the Haves are usually Pelagians, the Have-nots Jansenist. (Good and Evil are Riches and Poverty, a tree of misery propagating generation and death. William Blake)

But both views imply and are meaningless without the other, just as "Knock and it shall be opened unto you" implies and is meaningless without "None cometh unto me except the Father draw him."

1533   *or refuse*
    As individuals to choose

"The most aberrant man in Peri proclaimed his difference from his fellows as a boy by the unique act of hanging a charm on the back of a cousin whom he had seduced, so that the spirits could not punish her. In later life he used a vocabulary filled with obsolete words carefully collected from old men in different villages, and he laughed aloud at his sister's funeral. In all other respects he was very like his fellows; he married, his wife left him, he married again. He fished and traded for garden products, he engaged in eco-

148

nomic exchanges, he observed the name tabus of his affinal relatives as did all the other men in Peri. Another man in Peri was conspicuous on a different count—he had wept sincerely and lengthily for his wife when she died and he had kept her skull and occasionally talked to it. This made him a marked individual, unique in the experience of his kinsmen and neighbors. But in the bulk of his beliefs and practices, he differed not at all from all the other men in the village.

"Now let us consider a brief example of the kinds of individuals which we find among ourselves. Among two men of the same general personality-traits—i.e., both may be dominant, aggressive, originative, self-confident—one may believe in the Trinity and the Doctrine of Original Sin, the other be a convinced Agnostic; one may believe in free-trade, state's rights, local option; the other in tariffs, big navies, national legislation in social matters; one may be interested in collecting prints of early New York, the other in collecting butterflies; one may have a house done in Queen Anne furniture; the other have a house with a collection assembled from a dozen sources. . . . And so one could go through the entire range of possible tastes, and to complete the picture compare either of these men with a small clerk in a small city, whose only amusements are driving a Ford, going to the movies, reading the comic strips, whose house has been furnished in standard ugliness on the installment plan, and who is a Republican because his father was."

Margaret Meade. *Growing up in New Guinea.*

1543 *Each must travel forth alone*

"The choice was put to them whether they would like to be kings or king's couriers. Like children they all wanted to be couriers. So now there are a great many couriers, they post through the world and, as there are no kings left, shout to each other their meaningless and obsolete messages. They would gladly put an end to their wretched lives, but they dare not because of their oath of service."

Franz Kafka. *Aphorisms.*

1545 *The Nowhere-without-No*

Wir haben nie, nicht einen einzigen Tag,
den reinen Raum vor uns, in den die Blumen
unendlich aufgehen. Immer ist es Welt
und niemals Nirgends ohne Nicht:
das Reine, Unüberwachte, das man atmet und
unendlich weiss und nicht begehrt.

R. M. Rilke. *Duino Elegies.* VIII.

1548 *The landless knight*

"Landless knighthood, knighthood without a place in the territorial hierarchy of feudalism, seems to have been possible in Provence. The unattached knight, as we meet him in the romances, respectable only by his own valour, amiable only by his own courtesy, pre-destined lover of other men's wives, was therefore a reality."

C. S. Lewis. *The Allegory of Love.*

1552 *An unrobust lone fisher-king*

While I was fishing in the dull canal.
On a winter evening round behind the gashouse
Musing upon the king my brother's wreck
And on the king my father's death before him.

              T. S. Eliot. *The Waste Land.*

1553 *Each subway face*

This now is too lamentable a face for man;
Some abject louse, asking leave to be—cringing for it;
Some milk-nosed maggot, blessing what lets it wrig to
    its hole

This face is a dog's snout, sniffing for garbage;
Snakes nest in that mouth. I hear the sibilant threat.
This face is a haze more chill than the arctic sea
Its sleepy and wobbling icebergs crunch as they go—
This face is bitten by vermin and worms,
And this is some murderer's knife, with a half-pulled
    scabbard.
This face owes to the sexton his dismalest fee;
An unceasing death-bell tolls there—

I saw the face of the most smeared and slobbering idiot
    they had at the asylum;
And I knew for my consolation what they knew not:
I knew of the agents that emptied and broke my
    brother,
The same wait to clear the rubbish from the fallen
    tenement;
And I shall look again in a score or two of ages,

And I shall meet the real landlord, perfect and un-
harmed—
                                    Walt Whitman. *Faces.*

1566 *Their factory the champ-clos*

It is, perhaps, significant that the first American
writer to have an influence on European writers was
Edgar Allan Poe. The American literary tradition,
Poe, Emerson, Hawthorne, Melville, Henry James, T.
S. Eliot, is much nearer to Dostoievski than to Tolstoi.
It is a literature of lonely people. Most American books
might well start like *Moby Dick:* "Call me Ishmael."
Just as the James drawing-room is not a real drawing-
room, his Paris not a real Paris, his duchesses not real
duchesses, so Melville's sea is not a real sea nor his
whale a real whale. Most American novels are para-
bles, their settings, even when they pretend to be real-
istic, symbolic settings for a timeless and unlocated
(because internal) psychomachia.

Even the violence of the characters in "tough"
American novels seems a reaction of despair against
their loneliness. Afraid to be alone, they drink or kill.

1577 *And accurate machines begin*
      To concentrate its adults in

Speaking of his fellow commuters, he said: "There are
some who have just missed the same morning train for
twenty years."

1581 *How few pretend to like it*

"Where is the end of error? Is not all longing on earth
an error, this of mine first of all which craves the sim-

152

ple and the instinctive dumb life itself, ignorant of the enlightenment which comes through mind and art, the release through the Word? Ah, we are all brothers, we creatures of the restless suffering will, yet we do not recognize ourselves as such. Another love is needed, another love."

Thomas Mann. The Hungry.

1592 *Whose form is truth, whose content love*
Est ergo animae, vita veritas, sensus charitas.

St. Bernard.

1596 *The largest publicum's a res*
    And the least res a publicum

"Experience is the self-enjoyment of being one among many, and of being one arising out of the composition of many."

A. N. Whitehead. Process and Reality.

1600 *Where Freedom dwells because it must*
    Necessity because it can

For this quotation, and for the source of many ideas in the poem, v. *The Descent of the Dove* by Charles Williams.

1602 *And men confederate in Man*
"Mutual in one another's love, love and wrath all renewing,
We love as One Man; for, contracting our infinite senses,

We behold multitude; or, expanding, we behold as
   one."

                              William Blake. *Jerusalem.*

1629 *We seem altogether lost*

Anthropos apteros for days
Walked whistling round and round the Maze,
Relying happily upon
His temperament for getting on.

The hundredth time he sighted, though,
A bush he left an hour ago,
He halted where four alleys crossed,
And recognised that he was lost.

   "Where am I? Metaphysics says
   No question can be asked unless
   It has an answer, so I can
   Assume this maze has got a plan.

   If theologians are correct,
   A Plan implies an Architect:
   A God-built maze would be, I'm sure,
   The Universe in miniature.

   Are data from the world of Sense,
   In that case, valid evidence?
   What in the universe I know
   Can give directions how to go?

   All Mathematics would suggest
   A steady straight line as the best,
   But left and right alternately
   Is consonant with History.

Aesthetics, though, believes all Art
Intends to gratify the Heart:
Rejecting disciplines like these,
Must I, then, go which way I please?

Such reasoning is only true
If we accept the classic view,
Which we have no right to assert,
According to the Introvert.

His absolute pre-supposition
Is—Man creates his own condition:
This maze was not divinely built,
But is secreted by my guilt.

The centre that I cannot find
Is known to my Unconscious Mind;
I have no reason to despair
Because I am already there.

My problem is how *not* to will;
They move most quickly who stand still;
I'm only lost until I see
I'm lost because I want to be.

If this should fail, perhaps I should,
As certain educators would,
Content myself with the conclusion;
In theory there is no solution.

All statements about what I feel,
Like I-am-lost, are quite unreal:
My knowledge ends where it began;
A hedge is taller than a man."

Anthropos apteros, perplexed
To know which turning to take next,
Looked up and wished he were the bird
To whom such doubts must seem absurd.

1641 *That all have needs to satisfy*
And each a power to supply

Four men were discussing after dinner what part of
the body it would be most dreadful to lose. "I am a
novelist," said the first, "and if I became blind, I should
be ruined." "As a musician," said the second, "I can
imagine nothing more awful than becoming deaf."
The third, who was a surgeon, confessed that, if he
were to lose his hands, he would commit suicide. The
fourth remained silent. "Come on," the others urged
him, "what do you think?"

"Well, if you really want to know, I think the navel."

"The navel!" exclaimed the others in chorus, "but
why?"

"You see, I like to eat celery in bed, and, if I lost my
navel, where could I put the salt?"

1644 *Each a unique particular*

For I bless God for the Postmaster General and all con-
veyances of letters under his care, especially Allen
and Shevlock.

For my grounds in New Canaan shall infinitely com-
pensate for the flats and maynes of Staindrop
Moor.

For the praise of God can give to a mute fish the notes
of a nightingale

For I have seen the White Raven and Thomas Hall of
Willingham and am myself a greater curiosity
than both.

Christopher Smart. *Rejoice in the Lamb.*

1649 *Can live because we've lived*

A mother was horrified to come upon her small daugh-
ter shouting dirty words and spitting at the little girl
who lived next door.

"Whatever has come over you, Mary, to behave like
that? The Devil must have gotten into you."

"The Devil told me the dirty words," said Mary,
"but the spitting was a little idea of my own."

1649 *The powers that we create with are not ours*

The reverent fury of couples on the wedding night,
Jacob wrestling with a river demon at the ford,
St. Francis bleeding from the five stigmata of Christ:
Over and over again as our strength seems at an end
And enormous our wish to be defeated in the fight,
Our powers flow back to us and our courage is restored
In the battle-embrace of our loving antagonist,
That terrible enemy who wishes to be our friend.

1656 *To call thy true love to the dance*

Tomorrow shall be my dancing day
I would my true love did so chance
To see the legend of my play
To call my true love to the dance.
   Sing O my love, O my love, my love, my love,
   This have I done for my true love.

English Carol.

1657 *O Dove of science and of light*

> O God of science and of light,
> Apollo, by thy greate myght
> This litel laste book thou gye
> > Chaucer. *The House of Fame.*

1668 *Quando non fuerit, non est*
> v. Origen

1683 *And point our knowledge on its way*

> That learning, thine Ambassador,
> From thine allegeance wee never tempt,
> That beauty, paradises flower
> For physicke made, from poyson be exempt,
> That wit, borne apt high good to doe,
> By dwelling lazily
> On Natures nothing, be not nothing too,
> That our affections kill us not, nor dye,
> Heare us, weake ecchoes, O thou eare, and cry.
> > John Donne. *The Litanie.*

1684 *O da quod jubes, Domine*
> v. St. Augustine *Confessions.* Book X.

1704 *Our life and death are with our neighbor*
> v. St. Athanasius. *Life of St. Anthony.*

1705 *And love illuminates again*

> ". . . the more people on high who comprehend each
> other, the more there are to love well, and the more

love is there, and, like a mirror, one giveth back to the
other."

Dante. Purgatorio. Canto XV. 73-75.

*   *   *

For trewthe telleth that loue · is triacle of heuene;
Loue is the plonte of pees · and most preciouse of
    vertues;
For heuene myzte nouzte holden it · it was so heuy of
    hym-self,
Tyl it hadde of the erthe · flesshe and blode taken,
Was neuer leef upon lynde · ligter therafter
Tho was it portatyf and pershaunt · as the poynt of a
    nelde,
May non armure hit lette · nother hye walles.

William Langland.
Piers Ploughman. Passus I. 148-156.

1707 *The world's great rage*

Round the three actors in any Blessed Event
Is always standing an invisible audience of four;
The double twins, the fallen natures of Man.

On the Left they remember difficult childhoods,
On the Right they have forgotten why they were so
    happy,
Above sit the Best Decisive People,
Below they must kneel all day, so as not to be governed.

Four voices just audible in the hush of any Christmas,
Expressing their kinds of hopeful attention:
—"Accept my friendship or die"—
—"I shall keep order and not very much will happen"—

159

—"Bring me luck and of course I'll support you"—
—"I smell blood and an era of prominent madmen."

But the Three hear nothing, and are blind to even the
    landscape
With its rivers and towns and pretty pieces of nonsense:
For He, all father, repenting their animal nights,
Cries—"Why did she have to be tortured? It was all my
    fault";
Once more a virgin, she whispers—"The future shall
    never suffer";
And the New Life awkwardly touches its home, be-
    ginning to fumble
About in the Truth for the straight successful Way
That must always appear to end in some dreadful
    defeat.

MODERN SOURCES

Anton Tchekov	*Letters* (Translated by Tomlinson and Koteliansky)
Hans Spemann	*Embryonic Development and Induction*
Henry James	*The Spoils of Poynton*
	The American Scene
Margaret Meade	*From the South Seas*
Soren Kierkegaard	*Journals* (Translated by Alexander Dru)
Franz Kafka	*The Great Wall of China* (Translated by Edwin Muir)
R. M. Rilke	*The Duino Elegies* (Translated by Leishman and Spender)
	Letters to a Young Poet (Translated by H. D. Norton)
Werner Jaeger	*Paideia*
Nietzsche	*The Case of Wagner* (Translated by Thomas Common)
F. L. Wells	
C. M. Child	*The Unconscious: a Symposium*
Hyman Levy	*Modern Science*
Wolfgang Koehler	*The Place of Value in a World of Facts*
Thucydides	*History of the Peloponnesian War* (Translated by Crawley)

R. G. Collingwood	*Metaphysics*
Francis Steegmüller	*Flaubert and Madame Bovary*
Carl Jung	*The Integration of Personality*
T. S. Eliot	*Collected Poems*
Georg Groddeck	*The Book of the It*
R. S. & H. M. Lynd	*Middletown in Transition*
Vaslav Nijinsky	*Diary*
C. S. Lewis	*The Allegory of Love*
Thomas Mann	*Stories of Three Decades*
A. N. Whitehead	*Process and Reality*
Henry Adams	*The Education of Henry Adams*
Vachel Lindsay	*Collected Poems*
Paul Tillich	*The Interpretation of History*

THE QUEST

THE DOOR

Out of it steps the future of the poor,
Enigmas, executioners and rules,
Her Majesty in a bad temper or
The red-nosed Fool who makes a fool of fools.

Great persons eye it in the twilight for
A past it might so carelessly let in,
A widow with a missionary grin,
The foaming inundation at a roar.

We pile our all against it when afraid,
And beat upon its panels when we die:
By happening to be open once, it made

Enormous Alice see a wonderland
That waited for her in the sunshine, and,
Simply by being tiny, made her cry.

THE PREPARATIONS

All had been ordered weeks before the start
From the best firms at such work; instruments
To take the measure of all queer events,
And drugs to move the bowels or the heart.

A watch, of course, to watch impatience fly,
Lamps for the dark and shades against the sun;
Foreboding, too, insisted on a gun
And colored beads to soothe a savage eye.

In theory they were sound on Expectation
Had there been situations to be in;
Unluckily they were their situation:

One should not give a poisoner medicine,
A conjurer fine apparatus, nor
A rifle to a melancholic bore.

THE CROSSROADS

The friends who met here and embraced are gone,
Each to his own mistake; one flashes on
To fame and ruin in a rowdy lie,
A village torpor holds the other one,
Some local wrong where it takes time to die:
The empty junction glitters in the sun.

So at all quays and crossroads: who can tell,
O places of decision and farewell,
To what dishonor all adventure leads,
What parting gift could give that friend protection,
So orientated, his salvation needs
The Bad Lands and the sinister direction?

All landscapes and all weathers freeze with fear,
But none have ever thought, the legends say,
The time allowed made it impossible;
For even the most pessimistic set
The limit of their errors at a year.
What friends could there be left then to betray,
What joy take longer to atone for? Yet
Who would complete without the extra day
The journey that should take no time at all?

THE TRAVELER

No window in his suburb lights that bedroom where
A little fever heard large afternoons at play:
His meadows multiply; that mill, though, is not there
Which went on grinding at the back of love all day.

Nor all his weeping ways through weary wastes have
    found
The castle where his Greater Hallows are interned;
For broken bridges halt him, and dark thickets round
Some ruin where an evil heritage was burned.

Could he forget a child's ambition to be old
And institutions where it learned to wash and lie,
He'd tell the truth for which he thinks himself too young,

That everywhere on the horizon of his sigh
Is now, as always, only waiting to be told
To be his father's house and speak his mother tongue.

THE CITY

In villages from which their childhoods came
Seeking Necessity, they had been taught
Necessity by nature is the same,
No matter how or by whom it be sought.

The city, though, assumed no such belief,
But welcomed each as if he came alone,
The nature of Necessity like grief
Exactly corresponding to his own.

And offered them so many, every one
Found some temptation fit to govern him;
And settled down to master the whole craft

Of being nobody; sat in the sun
During the lunch-hour round the fountain rim;
And watched the country kids arrive and laughed.

THE FIRST TEMPTATION

Ashamed to be the darling of his grief
He joined a gang of rowdy stories where
His gift for magic quickly made him chief
Of all these boyish powers of the air;

Who turned his hungers into Roman food.
The town's asymmetry into a park;
All hours took taxis; any solitude
Became his flattered duchess in the dark.

But if he wished for anything less grand,
The nights came padding after him like wild
Beasts that meant harm, and all the doors cried Thief;

And when Truth met him and put out her hand.
He clung in panic to his tall belief
And shrank away like an ill-treated child.

THE SECOND TEMPTATION

The library annoyed him with its look
Of calm belief in being really there;
He threw away a rival's silly book,
And clattered panting up the spiral stair.

Swaying upon the parapet he cried:
"O Uncreated Nothing, set me free,
Now let Thy perfect be identified,
Unending passion of the Night, with Thee."

And his long suffering flesh, that all the time
Had felt the simple cravings of the stone
And hoped to be rewarded for her climb,

Took it to be a promise when he spoke
That now at last she would be left alone,
And plunged into the college quad, and broke.

THE THIRD TEMPTATION

He watched with all his organs of concern
How princes walk, what wives and children say;
Reopened old graves in his heart to learn
What laws the dead had died to disobey.

And came reluctantly to his conclusion:
"All the arm-chair philosophers are false;
To love another adds to the confusion;
The song of pity is the Devil's Waltz."

And bowed to fate and was successful so
That soon he was the king of all the creatures:
Yet, shaking in an autumn nightmare, saw,

Approaching down a ruined corridor,
A figure with his own distorted features
That wept, and grew enormous, and cried Woe.

THE TOWER

This is an architecture for the odd;
Thus heaven was attacked by the afraid,
So once, unconsciously, a virgin made
Her maidenhead conspicuous to a god.

Here on dark nights while worlds of triumph sleep
Lost Love in abstract speculation burns,
And exiled Will to politics returns
In epic verse that lets its traitors weep.

Yet many come to wish their tower a well;
For those who dread to drown of thirst may die,
Those who see all become invisible:

Here great magicians caught in their own spell
Long for a natural climate as they sigh
"Beware of Magic" to the passer-by.

THE PRESUMPTUOUS

They noticed that virginity was needed
To trap the unicorn in every case,
But not that, of those virgins who succeeded,
A high percentage had an ugly face.

The hero was as daring as they thought him,
But his peculiar boyhood missed them all;
The angel of a broken leg had taught him
The right precautions to avoid a fall.

So in presumption they set forth alone
On what, for them, was not compulsory:
And stuck halfway to settle in some cave
With desert lions to domesticity;

Or turned aside to be absurdly brave,
And met the ogre and were turned to stone.

THE AVERAGE

His peasant parents killed themselves with toil
To let their darling leave a stingy soil
For any of those smart professions which
Encourage shallow breathing, and grow rich.

The pressure of their fond ambition made
Their shy and country-loving child afraid
No sensible career was good enough,
Only a hero could deserve such love.

So here he was without maps or supplies,
A hundred miles from any decent town;
The desert glared into his blood-shot eyes;

The silence roared displeasure: looking down,
He saw the shadow of an Average Man
Attempting the Exceptional, and ran.

VOCATION

Incredulous, he stared at the amused
Official writing down his name among
Those whose request to suffer was refused.

The pen ceased scratching: though he came too late
To join the martyrs, there was still a place
Among the tempters for a caustic tongue

To test the resolution of the young
With tales of the small failings of the great,
And shame the eager with ironic praise.

Though mirrors might be hateful for a while,
Women and books should teach his middle age
The fencing wit of an informal style
To keep the silences at bay and cage
His pacing manias in a worldly smile.

THE USEFUL

The over-logical fell for the witch
Whose argument converted him to stone;
Thieves rapidly absorbed the over-rich;
The over-popular went mad alone,
And kisses brutalized the over-male.

As agents their effectiveness soon ceased;
Yet, in proportion as they seemed to fail,
Their instrumental value was increased
To those still able to obey their wish.

By standing stones the blind can feel their way,
Wild dogs compel the cowardly to fight,
Beggars assist the slow to travel light,
And even madmen manage to convey
Unwelcome truths in lonely gibberish.

THE WAY

Fresh addenda are published every day
To the encyclopedia of the Way.

Linguistic notes and scientific explanations,
And texts for schools with modernized spelling and illus-
trations.

Now everyone knows the hero must choose the old horse,
Abstain from liquor and sexual intercourse

And look out for a stranded fish to be kind to:
Now everyone thinks he could find, had he a mind to,
The way through the waste to the chapel in the rock
For a vision of the Triple Rainbow or the Astral Clock.

Forgetting his information comes mostly from married
men
Who liked fishing and a flutter on the horses now and
then.

And how reliable can any truth be that is got
By observing oneself and then just inserting a Not?

THE LUCKY

Suppose he'd listened to the erudite committee,
He would have only found where not to look;
Suppose his terrier when he whistled had obeyed,
It would not have unearthed the buried city;
Suppose he had dismissed the careless maid,
The cryptogram would not have fluttered from the book.

"It was not I," he cried as, healthy and astounded,
He stepped across a predecessor's skull;
"A nonsense jingle simply came into my head
And left the intellectual Sphinx dumbfounded;
I won the Queen because my hair was red;
The terrible adventure is a little dull."

Hence Failure's torment: "Was I doomed in any case,
Or would I not have failed had I believed in Grace?"

THE HERO

He carried every question that they hurled:
"What did the Emperor tell you?" "Not to push?"
"What is the greatest wonder of the world?"
"The bare man Nothing in the Beggar's Bush."

Some muttered, "He is cagey for effect.
A hero owes a duty to his fame.
He looks too like a grocer for respect."
Soon they slipped back into his Christian name.

The only difference that could be seen
From those who'd never risked their lives at all
Was his delight in details and routine.

For he was always glad to mow the grass,
Pour liquids from large bottles into small,
Or look at clouds through bits of colored glass.

ADVENTURE

Others had swerved off to the left before,
But only under protest from outside;
Embittered robbers outlawed by the Law,
Lepers in terror of the terrified.

Now no one else accused these of a crime;
They did not look ill: old friends, overcome,
Stared as they rolled away from talk and time
Like marbles out into the blank and dumb.

The crowd clung all the closer to convention,
Sunshine and horses, for the sane know why
The even numbers should ignore the odd:

The Nameless is what no free people mention;
Successful men know better than to try
To see the face of their Absconded God.

THE ADVENTURERS

Spinning upon their central thirst like tops,
They went the Negative Way toward the Dry;
By empty caves beneath an empty sky
They emptied out their memories like slops

Which made a foul marsh as they dried to death,
Where monsters bred who forced them to forget
The lovelies their consent avoided; yet,
Still praising the Absurd with their last breath,

They seeded out into their miracles:
The images of each grotesque temptation
Became some painter's happiest inspiration;

And barren wives and burning virgins came
To drink the pure cold water of their wells,
And wish for beaux and children in their name.

THE WATERS

Poet, oracle and wit
Like unsuccessful anglers by
The ponds of apperception sit,
Baiting with the wrong request
The vectors of their interest;
At nightfall tell the angler's lie.

With time in tempest everywhere,
To rafts of frail assumption cling
The saintly and the insincere;
Enraged phenomena bear down
In overwhelming waves to drown
Both sufferer and suffering.

The waters long to hear our question put
Which would release their longed-for answer, but.

THE GARDEN

Within these gates all opening begins:
White shouts and flickers through its green and red,
Where children play at seven earnest sins
And dogs believe their tall conditions dead.

Here adolescence into number breaks
The perfect circle time can draw on stone,
And flesh forgives division as it makes
Another's moment of consent its own.

All journeys die here; wish and weight are lifted:
Where often round some old maid's desolation
Roses have flung their glory like a cloak,

The gaunt and great, the famed for conversation
Blushed in the stare of evening as they spoke,
And felt their center of volition shifted.

EPILOGUE

Returning each morning from a timeless world
The senses open upon a world of time;
      After so many years the light is
      Novel still and immensely ambitious.

But translated from her own informal world
The ego is bewildered and does not want
      A shining novelty this morning,
      And does not like the noise or the people.

For behind the doors of this ambitious day
Stand shadows with enormous grudges, outside
      Its chartered ocean of perception
      Misshapen coastguards drunk with foreboding,

And whispering websters stealing through this world
Discredit so much literature and praise:
      Summer was worse than we expected,
      And now cold autumn comes on the water.

The lesser lives retire on their savings, their
Small deposits of starches and nuts, and soon
      Will be asleep or traveling or
      Dead; but this year the towns of our childhood

Are changing complexion along with the woods,
And many who have shared our conduct will add
    Their pinches of detritus to the
    Nutritive chain of determined being,

And even the uneliminated decline
To a vita minima, huddling for warmth
    The hard- and the soft-mouthed together
    In a coma of waiting, just breathing

In a darkness of tribulation and death,
While blizzards havoc the gardens, and the old
    Folly becomes unsafe, the mill-wheels
    Rust and the weirs fall slowly to pieces.

Will the inflamed ego attempt as before
To migrate again to her family place,
    To the hanging gardens of Eros
    And the moons of his magical summer?

But the local train does not run any more,
The heretical roses have lost their scent,
    And her Cornish Hollow of tryst is
    Swarming now with discourteous villains

Whom father's battered hat cannot wish away,
And the fancy-governed sequence leads us all
    Back to that labyrinth where either
    We are found or lose ourselves for ever.

Oh what sign can we make to be found? How can
We will the knowledge that we must know to will?
    The waste is a suburb of prophets,
    But few have seen Jesus and so many

Judas the Abyss. The rocks are big and bad,
And death so substantial in the thinning air;
    Learning screams in the narrow gate where
    Events are traded with time, but who can

Tell what logic must and must not leave to fate,
Or what laws we are permitted to obey?
    There are no birds; the predatory
    Glaciers glitter in the chilly evening;

And death is probable. Nevertheless,
Whatever the situation and the blame,
    Let the lips do formal contrition
    For whatever is going to happen;

Time remembered bear witness to time required,
The positive and negative ways through time
    Embrace and encourage each other
    In a brief moment of intersection;

That the orgulous spirit may while it can
Conform to its temporal focus with praise,
    Acknowledging the attributes of
    One immortal one infinite Substance,

And the shabby structure of indolent flesh
Give a resonant echo to the Word which was
    From the beginning, and the shining
    Light be comprehended by the darkness.